The Power of Relaxation

. . . .

DATE DUE

USING TAI CHI AND
VISUALIZATION TO REDUCE
CHILDREN'S STRESS

The
POWER
of
RELAXATION

....

PATRICE THOMAS

....

Redleaf Press
St. Paul, Minnesota
www.redleafpress.org

The exercises in this book are gentle and safe, provided the instructions are followed carefully. However, the publisher and author disclaim all liability in connection with the use of this information in individual cases. If in doubt, consult your doctor or medical adviser.

. . . .

Redleaf Press books are available at a special discount when purchased in bulk (1,000 or more copies) for special premiums and sales promotions. For details, contact the sales manager at 800-423-8309.

Published by Redleaf Press
        450 N. Syndicate, Suite 5
        St. Paul, MN 55104
Visit us online at www.redleafpress.org.

Library of Congress Cataloging-in-Publication Data
Thomas, Patrice Olympius.
   The power of relaxation : using tai chi and visualization to reduce children's stress / Patrice Thomas.— 1st U.S. ed.
      p. cm.
   ISBN 1-929610-37-8 (pbk.)
   1. Stress in children. 2. Stress management for children. 3. Mind and body in children. 4. Mind and body in children—Problems, exercises, etc. I. Title.
   BF723.S75T48 2003
   155.4′18—dc21
                                                                2003012810

CONTENTS

· · · · · · · · · · ·

FOREWORD

. . . .

Patrice Thomas has been a pioneer in promoting the importance of relaxation as a key life competence for young children. Building on the burgeoning literature on the long-term benefits of relaxation in countering the negative effects of stress, the author provides an important volume that will enable educators and parents to provide children with the skills to use relaxation as a means of enhancing their physical development, health, and well-being. Patrice describes in clear detail the basic elements of tai chi and progressive relaxation and provides a very timely and practical resource. It should prove to be a valuable tool for those seeking to address children's emotional needs and their skills for coping. Relaxation training is a key element in the development of resilient, competent children who will be well equipped to face and overcome the challenges of an increasingly stressful world. I congratulate Patrice Thomas and her publisher on an excellent addition to the literature.

Professor Alan Hayes
Dean and Head of Division
Australian Centre for Educational Studies
Macquarie University

ACKNOWLEDGMENTS

. . . .

Many people have helped me in the process of developing my work with children and writing this book. All of the following people understand the importance of honoring and empowering young children.

Noeleen O'Beirne had the vision and courage to incorporate relaxation classes into the special school of which she was the principal. This gave me my first opportunity to teach tai chi and relaxation to children, twenty years ago.

Virginia Field (my long-term tai chi teacher in the Blue Mountains, New South Wales, Australia) is an inspiration and guide who has encouraged me in my work with young children.

My dear friend Jennifer Sumsion has been an ongoing source of support and encouragement throughout the writing process.

José Pavis, my friend and confidant, through his enthusiasm and creativity has constantly encouraged me because of his belief in me.

My lifelong friends, Karen and Tim Logan, and their children, Katherine, Mark, and Joshua, have provided much love and support during the writing process. These three remarkable children appear throughout the book in photographs and as models for some of the illustrations. ›

My sister, Maureen, has been a constant source of support and a sounding board throughout the process of developing these exercises and writing this book.

The material presented in this book was developed with many groups of children and teachers over the past twenty years. I would like to thank them all for their enthusiasm and interest. In particular, I wish to thank Wendy Shepherd (director), Jennifer Eaton, Joanne Sykes, Eileen Kalucy, and the preschool children from Mia Mia Child and Family Studies Centre at Macquarie University for welcoming me into their setting and working so supportively and creatively with me. I would also like to thank Barbara Raczynsky and her pupils from the Kent Road Public School for their enthusiastic support of relaxation and tai chi.

I would like to thank my Australian publisher, Rodney Kenner, for having the vision to take this publication on and for his patience and support during some difficult times in bringing the manuscript to fruition. I would also like to thank Redleaf Press for publishing this U.S. edition, and especially my editor, Beth Wallace, whose support, patience, and boundless encouragement enabled this resource to come to fruition.

Finally, I wish to express my gratitude to my partner, John, who, from a place of unconditional love and patience, has helped me realize a dream in writing this book.

INTRODUCTION

This book has been a long time in the making. For many years it has been my dream to write a book about the use of relaxation techniques with young children. This dream emerged from the recognition of the need for children to learn to integrate the physical, mental, emotional, and spiritual parts of themselves.

I have always felt the need to spend time alone, where I can think, dream, reflect, and ponder. In my early life, I suppose this was my meditation time—what I like to call my "heart and soul" time. In this meditative and quiet space, I could bring myself back to a place of balance, replenish my energy, and bring a feeling of calm back into my life. My time alone helped me to stay in touch with my intuition, think through my problems, and find respite from the bustle of my family life and school demands—this time helped me to feel good about who I was. At no time in my school life were any opportunities for relaxation, meditation, or reflection time offered. The closest technique I can recall is a primary school teacher who used to allow us to wash our faces after lunch and put our heads down on the desk for five minutes—better than nothing, I suppose!

When, as a young teacher, I was introduced to tai chi, yoga, and meditation practices, I felt an immediate sense of enthusiasm. At last I had found some techniques where I could be part of a group, yet experience the benefits I had previously gained from my periods of time alone. Learning the techniques of breathing and moving meditation were a breakthrough in my life, as I was able to develop ways of being calm and centered in stressful situations. Although tai chi, yoga, and meditation have always remained regular practices in my life, it is the practice of tai chi that has made the strongest impact on who I am and how I live.

In the 1970s, during my early years of teaching, I was inspired by the children and staff of a "special school." (In Australia, "special schools" or "schools for specific purposes" served children with special needs, such as those with learning, physical, behavioral, and/or emotional disabilities. Today, special needs children are more frequently mainstreamed in regular primary or high schools, where they receive itinerant support from specialist teachers.) Noeleen O'Beirne, my dear friend and then principal of the school, had the vision and courage to incorporate relaxation classes into the school curriculum.

The young people attending this school (ages five to fifteen years) had suffered a range of abuse and neglect. These children were wards of the state and many had spent most or all of their lives in institutions, or moving from one unsuccessful foster placement to another. Many of the children were angry or violent; some had been expelled from the regular school system. All of the children at this school had emotional difficulties and severe learning disabilities. Traditional teaching methods did not work with these children, nor did the strict discipline practiced by previous school principals.

Noeleen had been my practice teaching adviser at this school some years earlier when I was completing my teacher training. I felt privileged to be a member of her teaching staff, and over the years we became great friends. Some of our colleagues at the school shared our enjoyment of tai chi, yoga, and meditation classes, so many of the staff joined classes after school together. It soon became an effective way to manage our stress levels as well as keep us all calmer and more balanced when dealing with the difficulties we faced in our very challenging workplace. Most of the teaching staff shared the same philosophies (about the importance of breathing, regular meditative practice, and so on) and we came to realize that tai chi, yoga, relaxation, visualization, and meditation practices would be worth introducing to the children attending our school.

We introduced the techniques gradually, based on careful planning and discussion at our weekly staff meetings. The teachers began introducing relaxation techniques (in one form or another) into their daily routine. For example, some classes would begin their day with a short meditation to music while the children were sitting at their desks; some teachers introduced simple breathing exercises, stretching, and simple chi gong movements as a way of providing a lesson break or before a transition from one activity to another (for example, before going outside for lunch or playtime). Other teachers decided to provide a regular relaxation session after lunchtime. Afternoons were always problematic at this school, as the children became more tired and irritable as the day wore on and their ability to concentrate on their schoolwork lessened. These simple inclusions to the school day were introduced carefully and planned thoughtfully—just as any other experience or lesson for children needs to be planned.

At this stage, a relaxation session involved asking children to lie on the floor, slowly inhale and exhale, and then participate in a visualization exercise (for example, taking an imaginary journey as their teacher told a visualization script or story).

Within a few weeks, relaxation became a valued part of the curriculum for the children and the teachers. There were upsets and obstacles along the way, such as some children refusing to participate at first because it was "stupid" or "weird." These children were simply asked to sit and watch until they were ready to join in. It was important to ensure that these children did not disrupt the other children who were enjoying their relaxation time. The "ripples" soon smoothed out and the children came to look forward to their relaxation sessions each day. Along the way, the children were learning some valuable life and relationship skills such as how to calm down using the breath; experiencing contentment and ease during and after gentle exercise and visualization; recognizing that other children and teachers had feelings and responses similar to their own; and the value of listening to other people and how this helps us to get to know and begin to understand others who might be very different from us.

Our principal, in consultation with her staff, the school authorities, and the house parents, decided to appoint one of the full-time staff as a "relaxation teacher." This role was taken on by one of our newer teachers who was experienced in the techniques of tai chi, meditation, and yoga. Each class had the benefit of a relaxation session with the "relaxation teacher" daily, as well as the above described times with their own class teachers. The program improved the quality of school life for children and teachers alike.

Although we did not undertake formal research on the relaxation program, we all noticed the improvements in the children's behavior in and outside the classrooms. Concentration levels improved and some children were able to stay on task for longer periods; there was also less teasing, bickering, and fighting in the playground. We also noticed individual children taking up segments of the relaxation program to use when they were outside of school hours. For example, I was teaching the "senior" class at the time and some of my pupils asked me to make audiotapes of relaxation music for them. The students reported that they listened to this music on their Walkmans before going to sleep or if they felt upset or annoyed. In class, some children would ask me if they could sit in our "relaxation" corner for a short time and listen to their tapes if they could feel themselves becoming frustrated, annoyed, or upset.

It was clear to me that these strategies were preferable to dealing with tantrums, fights, and explosions every day. I wished that someone had taught *me* these techniques when I was a child. These children found some peace, serenity, and improved self-esteem in their lives through our relaxation program. I saw the general school system as a whole failing these children, and I wondered why education curricula did not provide "heart and soul learning"—relaxation and awareness sessions for children of all ages. I am still wondering why this is not happening in more schools and child care centers today.

Tai chi and relaxation techniques continued to form part of my teaching practice as I moved to different settings. After my years in the special school, I took up a position as a lecturer in a teacher's college in Sydney. I used tai chi exercises as a way of providing a short break in lectures and tutorials. I would often begin a tutorial with a five-minute progressive relaxation or visualization exercise to help the students focus their attention and relax by getting in touch with their breathing. These simple techniques became popular and I was asked by my students over the years to make them a regular part of our classes.

My career then took me back into regular schools for several years. I worked as a special education teacher, providing support and expertise to classroom teachers of children with learning, emotional, or behavioral disabilities. I continued to introduce relaxation sessions in these settings and always received positive responses—from the children, the other teachers, administrators, and the parents. I was invited into regular classrooms to run relaxation sessions for the children and their teachers. These usually took the form of warm-ups, tai chi exercises, and relaxation and visualization exercises, although in some settings I introduced yoga movements as well. The teachers began to adopt these practices on a regular basis and commented that they noticed a positive difference in the behavior and the concentration levels of the children. Word began to spread and I was invited to other schools to present workshops on stress management for adults and relaxation for children.

I returned to university teaching and spent several more years teaching adults who were studying early childhood education. I continued my own studies and undertook several research projects that investigated stress in children and the benefits of relaxation in child care, preschool, and school settings. This ongoing research is part of my own university studies.

I continue to be invited as a guest speaker and consultant in the areas of stress management for staff and relaxation for children. I live in Sydney and in the Blue Mountains (an hour and a half drive west of Sydney), where I have my own studio and offer tai chi and relaxation classes for adults and children.

I have had enormous support for my tai chi lessons from early childhood, primary, and high school teachers; academics; school counselors; parents; medical and hospital staff; and especially from the children. Hundreds of people over many years have told me how much they have benefited from the relaxation practices I have shared with them.

WHY TAI CHI?

We live in a dramatically changing world and our children are being placed under more and more stress, be it at home, school, or in early childhood settings. The importance of developing relaxation techniques for young children is clear. Teachers and parents are under ongoing stress in their daily lives and often fail to acknowledge that children feel the effects of adult stress and the pressures of childhood (such as being cared for by a number of different people during their week including grandparents, child care centers, or before and after school care). Teachers report to me that they are frustrated and at a loss as to how to bring calm and quiet into children's daily lives. It seems that the old adage, "If you do what you've always done, you'll get what you have always had" applies here! Helping teachers find a way to bring balance into children's days is becoming a priority in these busy and stressful times.

I was heartened and inspired many years ago when I read this quote:

> It is our belief that a radical change in personal consciousness is necessary to change the course of humanity. We also believe that to open children to see these new ways of seeing the world is to make a loving and profound contribution to the betterment of our world. To expand awareness together with children is liberating, interesting and a great deal of fun. (Hendricks and Wills 1975, xvii)

Much research to date has focused on stress and stress management for adults. However, little has been done to study how we can teach holistic stress management skills to children at an early age, or to create programs for children that provide relaxation, self-awareness, and relief from stress. Many adults perceive a real gap in our education system. For example, Carol Jenkins (a writer and parent) says, "As a parent, I feel a great need for more information on mental and spiritual principles in a form easy to share with children" (Jenkins 1995, vii).

Tai chi exercises appeal to young children because they are simple and the movements they contain are flowing and enjoyable to perform. Children feel a sense of achievement and gain the benefits of "moving meditation" as they play with the movements. The body becomes relaxed as the breath and the movement become more coordinated. When the body learns to relax in this way, it is then possible for the children to participate in a progressive relaxation and visualization experience as they lie down on the floor. This provides much needed rest and replenishment in their day and appeals to their sense of delight and wonder as they share in the imagery and fantasy contained in the scripts and/or stories that the adult speaks aloud to them.

 WHAT'S IN THIS BOOK? This book combines gentle exercises (Tai Chi Ch'uan) and progressive relaxation and visualization techniques that are suitable for all children. Tai chi promotes strength, flexibility, suppleness, coordination, and good posture. Relaxation and visualization techniques teach children the value of stillness

and how to enjoy being calm, quiet, and inwardly reflective. Visualization techniques enhance children's abilities in developing imaginative, creative, and artistic habits. Most important, relaxation and tai chi are noncompetitive, nurturing techniques that children of all ages can enjoy.

The movements presented in this book are modified versions of simple chi gong exercises, brocades, or silk exercises, from the tai chi tradition. When adults attend tai chi classes, they learn warm-up exercises and introductory stationary exercises (for example, chi gong), and then progress on to a tai chi form. A tai chi form is a sequence of tai chi movements performed in a set order, moving in different directions and then returning to the starting position. The practice of learning tai chi sequences requires dedication, concentration, and commitment. It took me about three years to learn the Yang Style short form sequence to my satisfaction.

Learning a tai chi form is inappropriate for young children. However, I have found from many years working in early childhood and elementary school settings that children can gain benefit from and enjoy the stationary exercises derived from tai chi traditions. The exercises presented in this book have been modified slightly to suit the needs of young learners. They are simple and easy to remember. The exercises appeal to the children's sense of fun and playfulness. Traditionally, tai chi texts emphasize that we "play" tai chi rather than "do" it or "perform" it.

This book takes a holistic and ecological approach to working with children and is based on the following principles:

- ❖ The value of quiet and solitude
- ❖ The value of meditation and reflection (quiet time, prayer, visualization)
- ❖ The value of taking care of our bodies
- ❖ The value of intuition, imagination, and creativity
- ❖ The awareness of our natural way of being (relaxed and at ease as opposed to tense and anxious)
- ❖ The value of ecological awareness and kindness to the earth, its creatures and to each other
- ❖ The value of honest, caring relationships where deep feelings and visions are shared
- ❖ The value of acknowledging a range of cultures, traditions, and rituals

This guide provides teachers with a starting point for developing their own gentle exercise and relaxation programs for children. In this way, we can support the natural and healthy development of mind, body, and spirit.

CHAPTER 1

Stress in Children

*I*n the past twenty to thirty years, scientific and technological advances (for example, the Internet) have changed our society. Along with all the benefits the information and computer age has brought, the rapid change has also required the development of special coping skills for adults and children. Youngs (1995) discusses the impact of stress on the lives of adults and children, stating:

> Virtually no one feels free from stress these days, not even young people supposedly living "the best years of their lives." Childhood innocence is now almost impossible to sustain. The necessity of electronic media, disruption of the nuclear family and loss of the extended family, increased mobility and home-shifting, elimination of old forms of labour and new work and lifestyle alternatives, changing mores and shifting values in family life—all these are quickly altering the nature of childhood.

This is even more relevant today. Current figures from the Australian Bureau of Statistics (ABS) reveal marked increases in the numbers of children receiving child care—both formal and informal. Other recent social trends indicate that people are working longer hours (often as unpaid overtime) and that increasing numbers of households are experiencing financial stress. Additionally, one in four children does not live with both natural parents. Increasing numbers of the population (one in four people as of 1999—Australian Bureau of Statistics Yearbook) are experiencing mental illness. The three most common disorders are anxiety, substance abuse, and depressive disorders. Australia has one of the highest rates of youth suicide in the world, and alcohol and drug disorders are increasing in young people. The activity levels of Australians are decreasing. Fewer and fewer Australians are participating in physical activities and sports and more are experiencing the stress-related problems of a sedentary lifestyle (ABS 2002).

People in the United States experience similar pressures. Increasing numbers of American children are spending substantial amounts of time in child care. Children receive care from a variety of sources including in-home care by a relative or nonrelative, center-based care, or public school preschool programs (U.S. Department of Education 1999). Americans are also working longer hours and experiencing financial stress. Hayes (2003) discusses the "24/7" economy (twenty-four hours a day/seven days a week) and laments that the eight-hour work day and the living wage that it once promised have quietly vanished for American workers at every occupational level. Hayes believes Americans now have a lifestyle where work intrudes anywhere and everywhere and that workers have less time for everything. Many workers are described as being perpetually attached to work via a digital "leash"—pagers, cell phones, portable handheld devices, and laptops (International Labour Survey 1999).

In America in 2000, 22 percent of children lived with only their mothers, 4 percent with only their fathers, and 4 percent lived with neither of their parents. In 2000, 69 percent of American children lived with two parents as compared with 77 percent in 1980 (U.S. Census Bureau 2000).

More than 19 million American adults are affected by illness each year. These include anxiety disorders such as panic disorder, obsessive-compulsive disorder, post-traumatic stress disorder, and phobias (National Institute of Mental Health 2003). In addition, epidemiological studies reveal that up to 2.5 percent of children and up to 8.3 percent of adolescents in the United States suffer from depression (U.S. Department of Health and Human Services 2003). This research also reveals that depression onset is occurring earlier in life than in previous decades. Depression in young people often co-occurs with other mental disorders, most commonly anxiety disorder, disruptive behavior, substance abuse disorders, and with physical illness such as diabetes. In 1997, suicide was the third leading cause of death in ten- to fourteen-year-olds (National Institute of Mental Health 2003).

Obesity is still on the rise for American adults and children. One third of all American adults are now classified as obese (National Center for

Health Statistics 2000). Among children and teenagers ages six to nineteen years, 15 percent or almost nine million are overweight, which is triple the proportion in 1980 (National Center for Health Statistics 2000). This is obviously connected to the fact that as many as seven in ten Americans engage in little or no physical activity during their leisure time (U.S. Department of Health and Human Services 1999) and like Australians, are experiencing the stress-related problems of a sedentary lifestyle.

Hurried parents and teachers produce harried children. In today's fast-paced society, stress is becoming an ever increasing problem for young children. Teachers and child care workers see frustrated and exhausted children on a daily basis at child care and school. Many children are woken up in the early hours of the morning (for example, 5:30 or 6:00 A.M.) and are dropped off at one form of child care or another (for example, a neighbor, a grandparent or relative, or friends) before school care, long day care, preschool, occasional care, or a combination of some of these over any one week. After long days in child care settings, children are often collected late by parents who are tired and depleted from a long working day.

Many teachers complete tasks for children (for example, tie their laces, complete chores for them, clean up their belongings and their messes) because it seems to be easier and faster. By doing this on an ongoing basis, we are robbing children of precious practice in learning life skills and self-esteem. In addition, we are sending the unintentional message of disapproval to them (you take too long to tie your shoes, you don't button your shirt correctly, it's better if I just write your name for you, and so on). As a result, children are often left feeling inadequate, helpless, and despondent.

Pushing children to achieve too much at an early age can cause them to burn out. Some parents are so keen for their children to live up to their potential that they expect their children to be busy and occupied nearly every waking moment. Teachers, child care workers, and parents all need to find a balance between encouraging children to experience success in life and allowing them just to be children. Success at school and in other activities is important and worthwhile, but not at the expense of a child's well-being and happiness.

STRESS IN YOUNG CHILDREN'S LIVES

In addition, adults often unwittingly transfer their tension and stress reactions to children. Teachers and child care workers suffer from stress and burnout. This can result in negative interactions with children—ordering, yelling, and inconsistent messages being communicated (for example, loud noise is acceptable when the teacher is having a good day but forbidden if the teacher is in a bad mood). Stress derived from one setting can also be transferred to another. For example, some parents are employed in high-pressure positions and come home frazzled and short-tempered, often sending children to their rooms or outside to play rather than spending time with them. It is important to remember that many teachers and child care workers are parents too—so they spend time with children during the day and then face the rigors of family life at home. Many other factors contribute to the stresses in young children's lives, including the following:

- Long hours in child care, school, and after school settings
- Spending time with a number of caregivers
- Being apart from parent(s) for much of the day
- Blended families
- Bullying or teasing at school
- Parents' financial pressures
- Living at a frantic pace
- Loss of a parent, relative, friend, or even a pet through death
- Separation or divorce of parents
- The addition of a new baby to the family
- Moving house
- Abuse and neglect
- Family violence
- Learning difficulties
- Illness or hospitalization
- Excessive expectations from families
- Disability
- Cultural isolation

In addition, limited space for play and physical development is becoming a feature of Western life. Threats from others—for example, bullying and teasing from other children in parks and playgrounds, being robbed, assaulted, or even abducted—are all daily realities and may prevent parents from allowing children to experience free play in parks and gardens. Physical education and sports in schools are generally geared to performance and competition. Children can be pushed beyond their natural limits and some burn out at an early age. Others damage their young bodies; for example, hip and spine problems may result from some forms of gymnastics and dance. Other less agile children can suffer misery and ridicule at being forced to endure team games and sports that they have little natural inclination toward. Sedentary lifestyles, "junk food" diets, and the advent of video and computer games for "relaxation" are further contributors to stress in children. In recent times, the stress of children whose parents are refugees has been added to this list. These children may experience severe stress and trauma in the process of leaving their homes, traveling to a new country, waiting (perhaps in detention centers) for their applications for refugee status to be approved, and adapting to a new country.

STRESS AFFECTS CHILDREN

Stress from causes such as these may have a negative impact upon the health, development, and well-being of our children. If children are confronted with too many stressful situations or if the stresses are too severe, the strain can become too great for them to handle (Hendricks and Wills 1975; Honig 1986; Kersey 1986; Rickard 1996; Pearson 1998; Greenman 2002). Stress impacts adversely on children's physical, psychological, and emotional well-being, as well as their social skills and ability to concentrate and learn (Honig 1986; Elkind 1988; Romano 1992; Youngs 1995; Greenman 2002).

Some years ago, Jed, a boy in my composite primary class attached to a Children's Court, revealed to me that he had been expelled from a number of schools because he was always falling asleep in class and getting into trouble for fighting other children who teased him. His grades went down, he "acted out" even more, and he was eventually deemed an "uncontrollable" child by the State Child Welfare Department and placed in an institution. He disclosed to me that he was very "stressed" and frightened by his stepfather who would return home late and inebriated each night and beat Jed and his mum. Jed's way of coping with his stress and fear was to escape through his bedroom window and ride trains all night or seek shelter in abandoned cars after dark and try to sleep. When he chose to arrive at school (rather than abscond) often late, tired, and hungry, he was punished, which eventually led to his expulsion. The "system" was unable to cope with Jed's stress; his schools neither recognized his stress nor had programs to deal with it. Jed's life was disrupted and his life choices compromised by the punishment meted out to him for the way he responded to his circumstances.

Jed's story is an example of a child responding to extreme stress. But as recent brain research has demonstrated, even what looks like relatively small amounts of stress on a regular basis can permanently affect children's brain functioning and their ability to learn, problem solve, and get along socially with other children and adults. Teachers have very little control over the circumstances of children's lives outside the classroom. We can't prevent bad things from happening to children or eliminate harmful stresses from their lives. But we *can* look beyond the behaviors we experience in the classroom to their causes in children's lives, treat children with compassion and understanding, and teach them techniques to reduce and manage their own stress.

HOW CHILDREN COPE WITH STRESS

It is possible for most adults to verbalize their feelings and begin to take some positive action toward managing their stresses. Children, especially children under four years of age, often do not have the words to express their stresses, fears, and worries. Children react to stress and change in many ways (aggression, withdrawal, attention seeking, disobedience, difficulty sleeping or eating, bed wetting, irritability, sadness or tearfulness, changes in toileting habits, and bullying others as well as physical symptoms such as headaches or stomachaches). Many adults misinterpret children's stress reactions as inappropriate behavior. When adults are hurried, busy, or feeling stressed themselves, they often misinterpret the signals children are giving them. Teachers need to be observant of changes in children's behavior (such as being aggressive or throwing tantrums when they are normally placid). If children are being dealt with as if they are misbehaving—when, in fact, they are exhibiting a stress reaction—their stress, fear, or anxiety is not being recognized or managed. Children then have to deal with the additional stress of being reprimanded, yelled at, or punished and then may respond with more extreme acting-out behavior because they do not have words to express how they are feeling. There is a real risk of a downward spiral of stress reactions developing here. All too often, children are diagnosed with disorders such as Attention Deficit Hyperactivity Disorder (ADHD) or a variety of mental illnesses when they may in fact be expressing extreme stress or overstimulation.

I am not suggesting that difficulties with behavior and attention do not exist. After all, I have been teaching in regular and special schools for many years and I have seen a wide range of behaviors and syndromes. However, I am concerned with the recent trend of medicating children to slow them down and control their behavior, and to make them more compliant. Prescribing drugs to manage children's behavior is often done as a first resort rather than exploring more natural methods. Perhaps the prescription of medication is a simplistic answer to the problems of a complex world. While using psychotropic drugs may work to address children's behavior in the short term, we need to acknowledge that young children's brains are still developing and that the long-term physical, psychological, and emotional effects of these drugs have not been established. Are we teaching our children that problems can be "fixed" with drugs? How can we then help them to understand the dangers of addictive substances that create dependency and a plethora of other social and moral issues? At the very least, we could begin to use relaxation techniques alongside medication so that children learn self-coping and self-soothing skills as well as being slowed down by chemical, external means.

Clearly, children who are very stressed or sick need more help than educators or parents can provide. When children's stress levels are chronic and ongoing, it is best to refer them to a medical doctor and/or a school counselor, pediatrician, psychologist, or other professional. Educators, parents, and medical and welfare professionals can work together to help children regain their balance and healthy outlook on life. Children may need extra help when they exhibit the following behaviors:

- Are overly lethargic or depressed
- Seem to be more and more sad and are crying often
- Are increasingly aggressive
- Are experiencing ongoing eating problems

- Are suffering from fears and phobias that limit their everyday enjoyment of life
- Are increasingly unable to concentrate on school tasks
- Seem to be overly withdrawn

Relaxation sessions are not a blanket solution to the many educational, health, and behavioral difficulties experienced by our children in today's society—they are not intended to be. These sessions do, however, provide an alternative way of working with children that honors their individuality and their needs for respect, inclusion in decision making, and acknowledgment of their inner lives. Relaxation sessions are not expensive (they're free!), they cannot harm children, and they do not involve complicated behavior management or drug therapy programs. Surely relaxation is worth a try . . . we have nothing to lose and everything to gain!

WHAT DO WE WANT FOR CHILDREN?

When we think about what we really want for our children (whether we are parents or teachers), we are really visualizing a scenario of hope and optimism for the world and the future of children.

As early childhood professionals and people who care about children, we can have a positive impact on how children experience their world. The following are many of the dreams and wishes parents and teachers share for the children in their care:

- High self-esteem—for children to experience love and give love to others
- Feelings of empowerment, so that they can enjoy their achievements and realistically respond to disappointments when life doesn't "go their way"
- A sense of control over their lives so that they can cope with difficulties when they arrive and know that they have inner mechanisms to help them find calm and balance when life gets tough
- Joy, excitement, and pride in their achievements and confidence in who they are
- Vitality and physical energy—to be fit, well, and healthy so that they can spend time outdoors and attend school regularly

- Deep curiosity, enjoyment, interest, and enchantment with life (for example, appreciating the wonder of a rainbow, the beauty of a butterfly's wings, the artistry of a spider's web, and so on) so that they can be successful learners
- Satisfying relationships with children as well as adults of all ages (including the elderly) and knowing how to deal with conflict and upsets in ways that enhance relationships rather than damage them
- Character traits of fairness, acceptance, honesty, and empathy as well as learning that being a gentle and empathic, kind human being is a hallmark of inner strength and not a sign of weakness or inability to be resilient
- Appreciating that there is meaning and purpose to life and that each person's contributions are worthwhile and important (paid and volunteer work no matter what it is; how we care for and respect other people, animals, and the environment)
- Economic security, a place to live, and ample food
- Respect for and connections to heritage and culture
- Freedom to go anywhere and make life choices without fear of ridicule, attack, or prohibition
- Opportunities to reach full potential in order to achieve academic success and rewarding work later in life

Many of the above aims or wishes for children are reflected in the goals of multiculturalism in Australia (Office of Multicultural Affairs, cited by Milne 1997, 29). These goals are the following:

1. All Australians should have a commitment to Australia and share responsibility for furthering our national interests.
2. All Australians should be able to enjoy the basic right of freedom from discrimination on the basis of race, ethnicity, culture, or religion.
3. All Australians should have equal life chances and have equitable access to and an equitable share of the resources which governments manage on behalf of the community.

4. All Australians should have the opportunity to fully participate in society and the decisions which directly affect them.

5. All Australians should be able to develop and make use of their potential for Australian economic and social development.

6. All Australians should have the opportunity to acquire and develop proficiency in English and languages other than English, and to develop cross-cultural understanding.

7. All Australians should be able to develop and share their cultural heritage.

8. Australian institutions should acknowledge, reflect and respond to the diversity of the Australian community.

Though these goals come from Australia, similar goals are common to many peoples around the world. There are various ways to achieve the above wants and goals for children and society in general. Ultimately, each teacher (or center/school) working in collaboration with parents, needs to develop ways to best achieve these goals based on the needs, abilities, experiences, and backgrounds of the children they are working with. The techniques offered in this book as a "relaxation package" are one way that adults can begin to achieve some of the above goals. For example, using techniques and exercises from a range of cultures (tai chi, yoga, meditation and visualization, drawing mandalas, and so on) meets goals 7 and 8 in the above list. Ultimately, most of the goals we hold for children can be summed up in a broad definition of *health:* we want them to be healthy and to have healthy relationships with themselves, with other people, and with the world as a whole.

WHAT IS HEALTH?

Western society is slowly coming to understand that health is more than the absence of disease or illness. The Australian Bureau of Statistics (2001) comments on this change of perspective:

> Health is often defined in terms of its negative aspect (e.g., ill-health) and the key focus is the presence or absence of sickness, disease, injury, disability within the population. However, this is by no means the full story . . . The movement towards integration, both in terms of understanding health processes and responding to health problems, has paralleled growing interest

in alternative and holistic health treatments and approaches. In some areas people's health is being considered as a holistic phenomenon—relating to their whole person and context, rather than just to their physical and mental fitness.

Health really is about the presence of vitality—the ability to function and live our lives fully, actively, energetically, and harmoniously. Harmony and balance have always been central to the Chinese notion of health and well-being. The English word *disease,* or "dis-ease," which means lack of ease, harmony, and balance, begins to touch on this notion. Traditionally, Chinese families pay the doctor to keep them well and stop paying when the doctor has to treat them for a sickness. The practice reflects their belief that the purpose of medicine and doctors is to maintain the balance of the body and harmony of the soul. The practices of tai chi and relaxation also help achieve this balance and harmony. The word "chi" in Chinese means "energy" or "life force."

The holding together of opposites symbolized by the yin-yang symbol (reproduced here in the margin) is fundamental to the Chinese worldview, and has much to offer the West today. It provides a way of understanding the ebbs and flows of people's lives—in relationships, conflicts, work, and the surrounding environment—and can help people come to terms with, and have some control over, these forces.

The forces of yin and yang are as relevant in early childhood settings as in any other sector of life. We in the West can learn from the wisdom of the East and incorporate these concepts into daily life. As teachers, when we practice tai chi with children, we are not only sharing knowledge from an Eastern culture, we are facilitating a situation where they can experience the holistic health benefits of the movements. These benefits allow children to achieve the goals we design for them, and positive, life-enhancing habits for their futures are formed.

The sense of interconnectedness of all life represented by the yin-yang symbol also contributes to children's understandings of their interpersonal and social worlds. When children are relaxed and at peace with themselves, they are more open to developing positive relationships and will learn to listen to and appreciate others' viewpoints. This is the beginning of acceptance of people and situations that are different from what they are used to. The early seeds of acceptance of diversity, tolerance, and acceptance of others and their beliefs are able to be planted. The idea that we are connected to all things—to other people, animals, and nature—extends to children's appreciation of the uniqueness and value of all life forms. Learning to love and care for the immediate environment around them (home, preschool, the playground) will lead to a commitment to caring for the wider environment (forests, oceans, air, ecosystems, and so on) and the planet, later in their lives. Real health, then, is well-being on all of these levels:

- Physical
- Emotional
- Intellectual
- Spiritual
- Interpersonal
- Social
- Environmental
- Planetary

Tai chi, visualization, and meditation are now no longer as feared as they were, even ten years ago, as "New Age" or religious. They are mainstream practices for adults of many faith backgrounds in our contemporary, multi-cultural society. But what about children? They also need to find their own inner peace and contentment independent of the people and situations around them. Definitions of health are now beginning to include spiritual health as organizations and health care professionals are adopting more holistic approaches. Nurturing children's spirits is not a new concept in early childhood education. A hundred years ago Maria Montessori said it this way:

> If education recognizes the intrinsic value of the child's personality and provides an environment suited to spiritual growth, we have the revelation of an entirely new child whose astonishing characteristics can eventually contribute to the betterment of the world (Wolf 2000).

Nurturing the spirit is the responsibility of children's parents, but it is also the responsibility of early childhood teachers. Wolf (1996, pp. 8–9) poses the following questions to early childhood teachers:

- ❖ Who is to tell children that there is much more to life than accumulating more and more things?
- ❖ Who is to tell them that their real value as human beings lies within themselves and how they treat others rather than what they possess?

NURTURING CHILDREN'S SPIRITS

Wolf defines nurturing children's spirits as "helping them (children) experience some silence, cultivate their inborn sense of awe and wonder, care for the earth, practice peaceful resolution of conflict, be helpful and kind to their classmates, and honor people of races and religions other than their own" (p. 34). Wolf speaks of this as "spirituality," but it would be just as easy to call it "values education." Most early childhood teachers will recognize the items on Wolf's list as priorities in their classroom. Beginning a program of relaxation is one way of nurturing each child's spirit, and can form part of values education or peace education programs. Here are some ways that teachers can expand upon relaxation sessions to nurture children's spirits:

- ❖ Undertake acts of kindness: Ensure that you and your children make their presence felt in the world in a positive way. Encourage kindness and support for each other in the classroom. Help worthy causes, visit sick or elderly people, volunteer your time to help in a community project. Tell the children in your class that you are involved in these causes and think of ways you can involve the children (for example, sending letters and drawings to patients in an aged care facility or better still, arranging a visit to the home with your children).

- ❖ Recognize that children are also our teachers: When adults stop telling children how it is and start really listening to them, a wealth of insight can be gained. Provide times for children to share what they are thinking about. Questions such as these may come up:

  - How can I help the whale stranded on the beach near our school?
  - Will those children in the detention center die if they stay there?
  - Now that my aunty has cancer, does that mean I'll get it too? And, what can I do to make her feel better?
  - I wish my dog didn't die, he was my best friend.

You will tap in to the children's issues and concerns and also be able to hear the wealth of wisdom that comes from the rest of the class. This is where the seeds of compassion are planted.

- Be creative. Tell lots of stories. Make them up or read them from scripts or good children's books. Construct items that can be used in classroom routines—for example, mobiles, candle holders, lanterns, posters, paintings, or collages for the relaxation corner.

- Be real. Share your emotions with the children without burdening them. Let them know that you are feeling sad today because your cat is sick and has to have an operation at the vet; that you are excited because you are going overseas for your summer vacation; that you feel lonely sometimes; and so on. Your main role is to be a leader and supportive educator for the children in your care. However, your sharing helps children build a realistic view of people and understand that people are complex and experience a range of emotions.

- Be spontaneous. Celebrate the wonders of the present moment. Bring the children's attentions to the small miracles that happen each day—for example, a baby bird hatching in a nest, a new rose bud forming on the bush, the rainbow bending across the sky.

- Teach children with joy and lightheartedness. Show reverence, sadness, and respect when needed, but focus on the wonder of the human spirit and the natural world.

Developing People for the Twenty-First Century

The world our children will inhabit will be vastly different from anything we have experienced. Terrorist attacks are becoming a frightening reality in many countries, and threats of reprisals and war are daily new items. We are facing a time in history when issues of culture and diversity need to be explored with compassion and humanity. Early childhood educators can teach children about the world and its diverse people. What elements should form part of a person's toolkit to help them face the challenges of this century?

- *Tolerance*

Children need to learn about other cultures and other people in their culture. They need to appreciate that we subscribe to different religions, beliefs, and philosophies. Beginning to learn this at an early age will increase their chances of living in a peaceable world.

❖ *Freedom*

Children need to learn that each individual has basic human rights and that one of these is the right to worship or not, as he or she sees fit, provided it doesn't harm another human being.

❖ *Inquisitiveness*

This extends on the previous point and highlights the importance of children learning to find solutions to that which perplexes them and to speak out and explore issues that they sense are wrong. It is a basic human right to seek clarification of those things we don't understand.

❖ *Openness to learning*

It is our duty as teachers to help children learn something meaningful about other faiths, practices, and philosophies. Share books about different cultures and beliefs with children and invite parents and community members to your center regularly. In this way you are opening the door to appreciation of multiculturalism and acceptance of all people.

❖ *Reverence for and intimacy with nature*

When we become alienated from the natural world, our view of our place in the world becomes distorted. Respect and care for the environment comes from helping children develop a sensibility that they are one part of the web of life and are connected spiritually to the planet (mother earth).

❖ *Respect for indigenous traditions*

It is important to cultivate in children a respect for native cultures and their spiritual traditions. Indigenous peoples have in many instances maintained an intimate connection with nature. When young children learn about native cultures and traditions, they are also building their own spiritual connections with the natural world.

❖ *Compassion*

We teach children compassion by being compassionate ourselves. Learning to listen to children and validate their experiences communicates empathy and understanding to children. Allow children to observe you engaging in acts of compassion toward others as well as yourself.

How can teachers and other adults support children's development of these essential characteristics? Try these simple activities to help children notice these qualities in themselves and one another.

Creative Ways to Nurture Children's Spirits

A SILENCE GAME

When the children are involved in their activities and behaving well, provide them with a new challenge. Ask them to stop all talking and sit still for a few minutes. When the time is up, ask children what they heard in the silence. They may report such sounds as the teacher next door; a clock ticking; a bird singing outside; or their friend's tummy rumbling! Gradually increase the amount of silent time each time you play this game. This game teaches children that silence or quiet time does not come automatically in life and that we have to set aside special times to attain it.

CARE OF THE EARTH

Ask the children to finish the sentence, "I was kind to the earth today when I . . ." You may hear such responses as "put my lunch papers in the recycle bin," "watered the plants in my vegetable garden," "turned off the tap while I cleaned my teeth," and so on.

THE KINDNESS TREE

Place a small tree branch in a vase and place it beside a basket containing pieces of colored paper with flowers drawn on them. Each "flower" has a piece of ribbon looped through a hole in the paper. Whenever a child performs an act of kindness, place one of the flowers on the tree branch. At the end of the week, admire the kindness plant with the children.

JEWEL FLOATS

Create a calming toy by filling soda bottles with water, adding coloring if you wish. Have the children cut up scraps of foil and drop them in the bottle with glitter, old junk jewelry, and small trinket toys. Replace the cap securely and tape it closed. While turning the bottle, children can search for favorite objects. This is a soothing and calming toy. Encourage two friends to play with a jewel float together, especially if one of them is upset or sad.

BATHING BABIES   Help boys and girls to develop gentle interaction by bathing a baby doll and feeding it with a toy bottle. Fill a water tray with a shallow amount of warm soapy water and provide a place to dry and dress the dolls.

HUG A BUG   This encourages children to form friendships and to touch in an appropriate way. Play dance music, and when it stops, ask children to find someone to hug. Begin dancing again when the music resumes.

THE WORRY TREE   Bring a small tree branch to school as for the kindness tree. In this activity, use the colored paper to write down children's worries as they dictate them to you. The children may want to draw a picture of something they are worried about. Hang the worries on the tree so that the children can be free of them for a while. This is a good way to initiate discussion about what the issues are in your children's lives (for example, going to "big school" next year, a visit to the dentist, being teased by other children, and so on).

IMAGES   Show the children a ragdoll and ask them to describe what it looks like. Then ask them to pretend to be like the doll. Words like *floppy, bendy, loose, soft,* and *squishy* may be suggested. Link to how the children feel during a relaxation exercise.

MELTING   This is an enjoyable cool-down activity after a busy activity. Talk about the way ice cream melts and then have the children stand and demonstrate this to you.

BALLOONS   To help children learn how to breathe deeply for relaxation, ask children to expand (by inhaling) and contract (by exhaling) like balloons. Pretend the balloon is filling and emptying slowly. Demonstrate with a real balloon at first.

CHAPTER 2

Helping Children Manage Stress

As we saw in the last chapter, children experience all kinds of stress in their lives. For some children, their stress consists of everyday upsets and annoyances such as fighting over toys, being reprimanded by a teacher, or not being allowed to watch a favorite television program. For others, however, the stresses are more serious and ongoing: for example, living in poverty, suffering abuse, losing a parent, experiencing a traumatic event, and so on. We know what causes stress in children and the effects it has on them physically, mentally, socially, and spiritually. We also know what we want for children—health and well-being that encompass the physical, mental, emotional, spiritual, interpersonal, social, environmental, and planetary realms.

The first step is for teachers and parents to help children recognize what makes them stressed (for example, not getting their own way) and to notice how they are reacting to it (for example, crying, whining, or throwing a tantrum). It is important to encourage children to talk about their annoyances, worries, fears, and stresses—even at a young age. As children develop more competent language skills, they will be better able to do this. Discussing worries with a parent or teacher or other adult does help, but the stressors and stress reactions do not disappear. Adults can help children experience a sense of calm and help children detach from their worries by guiding them through some of the simple strategies outlined in this book. Learning how to "let go" of a problem or put it aside for a while is not teaching children to "forget about it and it will go away." It is about helping children to unwind and experience a marked reduction in the body's stress reactions.

Knowing all of the above, many teachers ask how they can guide and support children in positive and health-enhancing ways. The following are a few general suggestions that are easily incorporated into the curriculum:

    ❧   *Provide quiet and soft spaces in your classroom for retreat and reflection.* These spaces can range from relaxation mats for babies offering soft and soothing toys and play items to cubbies, houses, and cozy corners. These secret cubbies can be defined by curtains or soft material. They might be formed by bookcases or partitions or even the space underneath a table partially covered by a blanket. The possibilities for items to include in these quiet spaces are only limited by your imagination and that of your children. Use soft toys, materials with soft and appealing textures, relaxation books, and writing and drawing materials; have ambient or relaxation music playing in the background or just allow the child/children to enjoy the silence of some positive time alone or with another special person. These spaces can contain soft cushions of varying designs and patterns to bring a multi-cultural feel to this area so that all children feel accepted and included. Examples include Islamic and Indian patterns, patchwork and cross-stitched pieces, and materials from a range of cultural styles (for example, batiks, Hawaiian patterns, and so on). Ensure the same safety and hygiene standards in these areas as you would with any other planned activity.

    ❧   *Ensure that you are providing a balance between indoor and outdoor time.* Revisit your outdoor spaces and if the climate allows, design some quiet spaces where the children can enjoy some time away from structured activities or simply be on their own for a while. Here are a few ideas: A blanket under a tree where children can "lose" themselves in the rhythmic sounds of a wind chime; a quiet sitting nook with child-sized chairs and a reading/drawing table; a secluded seat near a bird feeder to allow for some time to observe the wildlife that visits the playground; a bench near a covered pond or aquarium so that the child may enjoy the tranquility provided by some fish; an outside reading area where children can lie on mats and cushions and look through their favorite books; a children's garden where they can dig, weed, and water (under adult supervision if necessary).

❖ *Provide an ongoing variety of open-ended materials and activities.*

Many children become frustrated and "testy" if their creative talents are being stifled. Too much structure and the same old activities become as boring for children as they do for adults. Provide choices for children by setting out a range of good-quality drawing, painting, modeling, craft, construction, and other play items. Allow sufficient time for children to complete these activities. Provide opportunities for those children who wish to continue with their projects to do so, whether this involves moving on into the afternoon session, the next day, or over several days or weeks.

❖ *Limit the number of transitions that occur in a child's day.*

Examine your schedule and ensure that it offers children long blocks of uninterrupted time to immerse themselves deeply in play and work, and doesn't require them to transition frequently from one activity or focus to another.

❖ *Bring the concept of ritual into any transitions in a child's day.*

Greenman (2002) highlights the importance of providing comforting routines and rituals for children under stress. Relaxation techniques can become a welcomed part of young children's days. For example, extract one or two favorite tai chi movements to do before morning snack or lunchtime. Accompany the arrival and departure transition times with familiar relaxing and peaceful music.

❖ *Provide opportunities for children to monitor their own stress levels and make choices about the activities they are undertaking.*

For example, if a child notices that he is becoming hot, tired, and "fed up" running around on the playground, assist him by offering a choice of quieter, restful activities. The optimum situation is, of course, when children can remove themselves from a stressful situation into a nonstressful or less-stressful one. Given frequent opportunities, children can learn to become more proactive in the ways they manage their own stress. This is beneficial for becoming a coping and resilient adult.

> ❧ *Provide conflict resolution strategies and support children in using them when needed.*

See *Peace Education in Early Childhood* by Rosemary Milne (1997) for further details.

> ❧ *Provide a relaxation session each day as well as including relaxation techniques as short breaks during the day or at transition times.*

USING TAI CHI AND RELAXATION WITH CHILDREN

There are many books available that provide useful information on the above strategies. *The Power of Relaxation* addresses the final one—providing relaxation as a way of reducing and managing stress in children.

This book introduces a range of simple techniques that enable children to deal with their stresses more easily. The exercises can easily be used at early childhood centers, schools, and homes, with children of most ages. They provide children with inner peace, the security of a daily relaxation routine, and well-being. The book concentrates on the gentle exercise of tai chi with children; however, other forms of gentle exercise could be substituted, such as stretching exercises or simple yoga. Teachers and parents need to use their discretion and knowledge of their children and the kinds of exercises that are appropriate to different age groups. Here I have focused on simple (and in some cases modified) tai chi movements after years of trialing them with a range of age groups across varied settings. The tai chi exercises are easy to learn, repetitive, and gentle. They also appeal to children's sense of fun and imagination as they easily relate to the symbolism of the names and movements in each of the exercises (for example, "the peaceful dove opens its wings").

Tai chi and relaxation can be readily integrated into early childhood and school curricula. For example, tai chi movements can be used for short transitions or lesson breaks. Tai chi can also form a strong component of physical education experiences. Relaxation and visualization sessions can also be incorporated into the creative arts and serve as innovative ways to explore drama, storytelling, writing, and art experiences.

Using tai chi and relaxation, teachers can help children learn to recognize stress and how their bodies and minds react to it. This can be done with young children right through to teenagers. Children can learn to recognize when they are feeling angry, sad, upset, tired, and annoyed, and the accompanying body signals. Once they have learned some ways to use relaxation to help them with these symptoms and feelings, they can begin to see the benefits of the techniques and will want to keep using them. It is worthwhile to ask children how they feel before the commencement of the session (for example, *okay, bad, tired, sad 'cause Tom hit me,* and so on) and then compare these responses with how the children feel after the session (*light, happy, like a feather, soft,* and so on).

Over the years, I have used tai chi movements with children with a range of special needs. Children with physical disabilities find that they can do most of the movements and enjoy the feelings of accomplishment that result. Children with vision and hearing impairments find tai chi movements enjoyable and easy to perform; little help from an adult is needed. Children in wheelchairs can participate in the movements using the upper body and arms. I have conducted tai chi and relaxation sessions in hospital rooms with small groups of children and their parents. Some children even participated while sitting up in bed!

In our rich, diverse, multicultural society, tai chi is one form of movement and exercise that acknowledges the traditions of an Asian culture. One Asian parent (having just arrived in Sydney) told me how pleased she and her husband were to hear that their daughter would be learning tai chi in the preschool class where I was helping out. The mother explained how important it was for her daughter to experience a familiar and loved practice from her birth country. The practice helps to enrich all our lives.

HOW RELAXATION HELPS CHILDREN

- Relaxes the body
- Quietens the mind
- Allows the child to simply "be"
- Provides rest and rejuvenation
- Opens the children's imagination and creativity
- Allows children to feel good about themselves
- Provides time-out and solitude
- Helps coping skills
- Develops self-awareness
- Provides enjoyable, uplifting experiences

    (Rickard 1994; Thomas and Shepherd 2000).

WHY TAI CHI?

Tai chi and visualization techniques, done either in a small group or individually, are effective tools for reaching the relaxation state in people of all ages. For children to achieve what we want for them, they need to be able to have strategies for becoming calm, clear, and self-aware. Children learn better when they are not stressed-out, and they can manage their problems and conflicts more positively when they think through their responses calmly. A regular spiritual practice such as tai chi (yoga, meditation) helps many adults to access their own center and place of inner stillness, and supports them in achieving their life dreams and aspirations. Relaxation skills go a long way toward allowing this to manifest for children as well. If we want physical and mental health for our children as they grow up, teaching them techniques to manage stress, seek calm and clarity, and keep their minds and bodies flexible is a good way to start.

Uhlmann (1997, p. 24) tells us that "perhaps the greatest gift meditation brings children is the ultimate realisation of a secure haven within themselves, a safe, peaceful inner-zone where their own truth dwells." This truth will guide children toward behavior that supports rather than damages them.

The general benefits of tai chi and chi gong exercises include the following:

- Developing the natural potential of the body toward health and fitness
- Finding coordination in movement
- Improving balance
- Increasing flexibility
- Developing muscle strength
- Improving posture
- Balancing and clearing the mind
- Sharpening the mental faculties
- Increasing sensitivity and awareness
- Providing a channel for releasing emotional energy
- Improving memory
- Increasing alertness
- Improving quality of sleep
- Increasing oxygen supply and improving blood circulation

- Improving heart and lung function
- Increasing appetite
- Improving digestion and absorption of nutrients
- Strengthening the immune system

Jahnke (2002, p. 226) says this about chi gong:

> Physiologically, the blood circulation is increased by Qigong, the delivery of oxygen and nutrition is accelerated, lymph moves more vigorously, immune cells are mobilized, and neurotransmitters associated with the self-repair capacity of the human system are produced and circulated. If there is a particular body part or function that needs healing, the use of movement, breath, massage and mind focus can help direct Qigong benefits to it.

Khor (1993) categorizes the overall benefits of tai chi under the heading of "personal development and growth." He emphasizes that body control and self-discipline are the first steps toward growth and development. This physical control and stability, relates Khor, is reflected on the mental level for individuals in the form of a balanced mind, capable of making rational decisions and taking responsibility for their lives. According to Khor, through the moving meditation of the exercises and the various forms, tai chi stimulates and clears the mind, sharpens the mental faculties, and improves sensitivity and awareness. Further, the emotions are stabilized through correct breathing practice, proper balance, and a positive mental state. Tai chi is thus really about restoring a balance between the body, mind, emotions, and spirit.

When children "play" tai chi they are bringing balance into their day. The calm feelings and sense of ease and self-control the exercises provide for children help them to appreciate the value of quiet, gentle movement. For many children, these times are in stark contrast to the rest of their days where they are subject to constant noise, activity, busyness, and routine. The effect of the latter is stress, tension, upset, and discomfort. Tai chi exercise provides the opposite of these feelings and brings children back to a state or equilibrium where they can feel happy, relaxed, rested, and content.

PRACTICING WHAT YOU TEACH

The next chapter will discuss the specifics of planning and carrying out a relaxation program with young children. Before embarking on a relaxation program with your children, however, it is important to ensure that relaxation is already a part of your life. This means integrating relaxation as a way of being in your life rather than just seeing it as another technique that can be used to "fix" yourself and the children when stress becomes too much. Many educators and parents want their children to learn to relax but fail to see how their own stressful behaviors affect those around them. There are many ways that teachers can develop an ecology of relaxation in their own lives. The suggestions here fall into three broad categories:

❖ Developing a relaxed way of being
❖ Using specific relaxation techniques
❖ Creating a calm work environment

Developing a relaxed way of being

In order to develop a baseline of serenity and calm in your daily life, try to pay attention to each of the following areas throughout the day, whether at work or at home:

❖ Breath
❖ Voice
❖ Posture
❖ Language
❖ Empathy

BREATH

Breath is intrinsically linked with relaxation. A racing breath often equals a racing mind.

Take a moment or two right now to notice your breathing. Is it relaxed and easy or is it short and fast? Are you grabbing in short breaths? Are you holding your breath when tense? Notice if your neck and shoulder muscles are contracted and tight—this restricts your breathing. Use slow inhalations and exhalations to bring your breathing back into balance to achieve a state of calm. The breath should not be forced and should come naturally.

You will soon begin to understand the meaning of the term "breath is life!" Correct breathing increases your energy and reduces stress. Continually remind yourself to return to relaxed and comfortable breathing throughout the day.

Voice is another indicator of either a calm or uptight state. Often we do not realize that we speak too quickly or too loudly much of the time. Notice whether your voice is calm and relaxed or jarring to those around you. Work on developing a calm, even speaking voice.

VOICE

Good posture alleviates muscular strain. Developing a comfortable, aligned posture will help you move through the day with more ease and confidence. Notice your posture right now: is it relaxed and in alignment? Correct posture facilitates relaxed breathing and helps us to manage pain. Your body will eventually develop good postural habits if you begin to train it.

POSTURE

When standing, keep your knees loose (don't lock them). This gives you some flex and spring. Keeping your pelvis slightly forward and your stomach tucked in will help prevent pain in the lower back. To visualize proper alignment, imagine a silken thread coming out of the top of your head from which your head is suspended. At the same time, hold your feet slightly apart and imagine that you have another silken thread coming out of the base of your spine, connecting you to the center of the earth. In this way you will feel centered with your feet planted firmly on the ground, rather than feeling "fuzzy" with your "head in the clouds." When sitting, try to use an ergonomic chair with a firm back and support that enables you to maintain the lumbar curve in your lower back. Ensure that the chair is set so that your knees are level when your feet are flat on the floor. Try to keep your legs uncrossed to facilitate circulation (Anderson 1997). Consult a chiropractor or an osteopath, or undertake classes in Feldenkrais, yoga, or Pilates to learn more about the importance of posture to well-being and health.

LANGUAGE   Negative language causes disharmony and tension. Try to eliminate the language of negativity, judgment, and criticism from your vocabulary. Avoid sarcasm, moralizing, giving orders, criticizing and lecturing, labeling children, using You-messages, and interrupting or finishing children's sentences. Use the language of encouragement and optimism around children. Be aware that general praise can become trite and meaningless if overused. Try to limit the number of times you use stock phrases such as "Good children," "Nice job," and so on. Be genuine and specific when you compliment or affirm children's behavior or responses so they know specifically what you mean.

For example, the following are some common examples of negative language used with children:

"Don't throw sand again! You know it hurts people." (ordering)

"You silly boy—you should know better!" (criticizing, a you-message)

"Big boys of four don't cry; stop being so dramatic." (lecturing, minimizing, moralizing)

"If you do that one more time I'm taking it from you." (threatening, ordering)

"Stop making so much noise." (ordering)

"You are just too naughty for words." (criticizing, labeling, a you-message)

"No, you can't play with the bikes right now—how many times do I have to tell you?" (ordering, criticizing)

"I didn't know I was teaching a class full of monkeys." (sarcasm, labeling)

The following are the same examples rephrased in an optimistic, encouraging way:

"Use the spade to move the sand."

"Use words to tell Sam you want the spade back. You could say something like, 'I want the spade back, please.'"

"Remember to take care when . . ."

"It's okay to cry. Tell me what happened when you fought with Sarla."

"Remember, we use quiet voices inside."

"When children misbehave, I feel sad. I'd like people to listen to me."

"We play with bikes after lunch. Right now, you can choose between the block corner and the water play table."

"We treat each other kindly at kindergarten."

"Patrice feels sad when children in her class forget the rules. Let's all listen so we can finish the story."

"It makes me happy when everyone comes to the mat for our story as soon as I ask."

"Nathalie, you were kind to Josh when he fell."

"Rani, you tried really hard to tie the laces on your runners—you'll be able to do it all by yourself soon."

EMPATHY

Showing care, consideration, thoughtfulness, and kindness to others reaps its own rewards. Model tolerant and respectful behavior to those around you. It's important to treat children and other adults in the room the way you want children to treat you and one another. Remember that they are learning how to be in the world from everything they see and hear you do. This is achieved through using a quiet, calm voice; positive language; and communication techniques such as active listening and I-messages.

Sometimes people sabotage their intentions to introduce positive changes into their daily lives by saying one thing and then doing the opposite. We all need to commit to a philosophy of relaxation that integrates all areas of our lives. Making a heart and soul commitment to relaxation and self-awareness will help ensure that it becomes a much loved and enjoyed part of our overall approach to life.

Using specific relaxation techniques

Once you've established the basis for a serene disposition by paying attention to the factors above, you can expand upon it with practices that further relax and calm you. Relaxation techniques can transform stress into vitality when practiced on a daily basis. Try to incorporate some of the following ideas into your daily routines.

- Use breathing techniques
- Make time for meditation, prayer, or reflection
- Get regular exercise
- Maintain good nutrition
- Drink sufficient water
- Manage your time well
- Use affirmations
- Nurture yourself

BREATHING TECHNIQUES

Relaxation research (Farhi 1996) shows that breathing techniques are the most readily accessible resource we have for creating and sustaining our vital energy. Breathing practice can help ward off disease by increasing our immune system's functioning and by lowering blood pressure and cholesterol levels. There are many simple breathing exercises that take only a few minutes each day but have lasting effects on one's health. Either of the following books can help you get started:

The Breathing Book, by Donna Farhi. 1996. New York: Henry Holt.
Breathe Better, Feel Better, by Howard Kent. 1997. Allentown, PA: People's Medical Society.
Learn to Relax, by Mike George. 1998. San Francisco: Chronicle.

MEDITATION, PRAYER, OR REFLECTION

Insight and connection to intuition (inner knowing; soul self) can be developed through the regular practice of a meditative discipline such as prayer, reflection, and visualization. Through these practices we can tap into the power, richness, and creativity of our inner world. Many people who follow a faith already take time out to pray and reflect. This practice helps them to cope with the challenges of life. People do not need to follow a religion to experience the benefits of meditation and reflection. One way to learn more about prayer and meditation is to join a meditation class or prayer group; you might also want to consult a book on meditation, such as one of the following:

Wherever You Go, There You Are, by Jon Kabat-Zinn. 1995. New York: Hyperion.
The Blooming of a Lotus, by Thich Nhat Hanh. 1999. New York: Beacon.

Another part of bringing a calm way of being into your life is to provide sacred time and space for yourself. Spending time alone, surrounded by objects that enhance the atmosphere of relaxation (candles, flowers, quiet music), helps us nourish ourselves and "fill the well" before it becomes too depleted. Set aside a relaxation space in your home and spend time alone there each day if possible.

REGULAR EXERCISE

Exercise (for example, tai chi, yoga, walking, swimming, gardening) practiced for at least twenty minutes three times a week relaxes our bodies and minds. Exercise helps to burn off "stress chemicals" that can accumulate in our bodies. Regular breaks for walking, moving, or stretching throughout the day are also beneficial.

The ongoing practice of relaxation exercises, such as those presented throughout the book (progressive muscle relaxation, for example), can also bring peace and contentment into our lives. You can practice these alone, by listening to a tape, or by joining a group.

GOOD NUTRITION

A healthy, balanced diet consisting of fresh food helps your body combat the toll that stress can take. Consult a physician or dietician or simply buy some books on good nutrition to put good eating habits in place. Avoid resorting to convenient "junk" foods when experiencing stress. There are many resources available to help you change your nutritional habits. You might wish to consult one of the following books:

8 Weeks to Optimum Health, by Dr. Andrew Weil. 1998. New York: Fawcett.
Eating Well for Optimum Health, by Dr. Andrew Weil. 2001. New York: Quill.

DRINKING
SUFFICIENT
WATER

Drinking clean, purified water enhances many bodily functions, including the way you react to stress. Lethargy and fatigue often result from too little water consumption. Hydration, or adding more water to your diet, assists in maintaining calm feelings as well as preventing many health problems (for example, constipation, headache, and hypertension). A minimum of 6 to 8 glasses of purified water each day is the usual recommendation, but these days many people are trying to consume more, as much as 2 to 3 liters per day. Consult a medical or health professional for advice.

TIME MANAGEMENT

Positive time management helps us achieve our goals and manage ourselves in a calm and productive way. Stress is often caused when we "manage by crisis." Relaxed people plan their days so that they are not burdened by inflexible deadlines and relentless schedules. Taking time out for ourselves to relax and refresh each day is important.

POSITIVE
AFFIRMATIONS

Affirmations can help you achieve your aspirations in life. Affirmation (or autosuggestion) is a technique that involves the repetition of carefully chosen words or sentiments. We can achieve the results we desire in life (both immediate and long term) and change unproductive habits and stress responses through the use of affirmations. The repetition of these positive statements influences the subconscious and becomes self-fulfilling. For example, see the following:

"I am now calm and relaxed."

"I now eat healthy, fresh food every day."

"I am a creative and talented person."

"I exercise three times a week to keep my body and mind in good shape."

"I am organized and efficient at work."

To learn more about using affirmations, you might consult one of the following books:

You Can Heal Your Life, by Louise Hay. 1987. Carlsbad, CA: Hay House.
Working Inside Out, by Margo Adair. 1984. Berkeley, CA: Wingbow Press.

Self-nurturing is an essential part of transforming stress and bringing happiness and calm into your life. Explore ways to de-stress during the day (for example, taking a brief walk outside or stretching for five or ten minutes every so often) or at the end of the day (for example, a warm bath with fragrant oil and candles after a busy day).

NURTURE YOURSELF

We can also learn to transform stress in the work environment. Try to include some of the following suggestions in your everyday environment at work:

Creating a calm work environment

- Remove clutter from your workspace
- Organize your day
- Provide yourself with functional and comfortable furnishings
- Create workable systems for getting things done
- Replace caffeinated beverages, such as colas or coffee, with water or herbal teas
- Play music
- Take breaks
- Reward yourself
- Separate work from your home life and personal time
- Communicate with those around you
- Make technology work for you

Remove all clutter from workstations and other areas. Clutter creates mental confusion. Organized, tidy workstations help us to achieve our goals and efficiently attend to the tasks at hand.

UNCLUTTERED WORKSTATIONS

BE ORGANIZED

Try to spend a few minutes each morning to plan your day and set priorities. During this time, you can order your desk, set the day's objectives, and gather your thoughts. Deep-breathing exercises are also useful at this point.

FUNCTIONAL AND COMFORTABLE FURNISHINGS

Include a balance of comfortable as well as functional furnishings in your work environment. This is especially important if you work with children. As well as the necessary desks, shelves, cupboards, and filing cabinets, introduce soft, aesthetically pleasing furniture items. These can include lounge chairs, cushions, soft fabrics and hangings, and any other elements that bring a relaxing feel to the indoor environment. The following are some other suggestions for humanizing your workspace:

- Introduce aesthetically pleasing decorating items. We can bring a stale environment alive with beautiful objects from home. Simple additions such as a vase of fresh flowers or light, flowing curtains or hangings can lift our spirits on busy, tiring work days.
- Bring environmental posters into the workplace. Unless we work directly with children, we may not find an opportunity to enjoy a visualization exercise during the day. We can, however, bring posters and prints (for example, rainforest, beach, mountains, desert, and so on) that remind us of the restful and healing power of nature.
- Crystals, gemstones, and rocks can bring feelings of restfulness and relaxation into work and home environments. Quartz crystal is a powerful tool for use in protecting areas at work and home. Gemstones and rocks bring elements of nature into otherwise sterile work environments.
- Wind chimes invite "the spirit of the wind" into our surroundings. Wind chimes soothe the soul and are said to protect and heal the buildings where they are placed. A gentle breeze or a light touch can bring forth their delicate sound.
- Aromatherapy techniques, such as using oil burners, fragrant sprays, and essential oils, can heal the body, uplift emotions, and relieve tension (Nagy 1995). Do not leave a naked candle flame

burning near children. It is also important to be aware of the contraindications for some essential oils; for example, do not use clary sage and some other oils during pregnancy. Some people are allergic to fragrances and essential oils, so care is necessary here. If you experience a negative reaction to any particular oil or fragrance, cease using it. If you decide to use aromatherapy with children, seek parental permission first and ensure you have up-to-date medical information relating to children's allergies or illnesses (for example, asthma and sinusitis).

❧ Bringing plants and flowers indoors transmits the tranquility of the natural world. When we contemplate the colors, textures, fragrances, and shapes of plants and flowers, we relax the tight focus that life often imposes upon us.

Ensure that your work routines are efficient and help you achieve your relaxation goals. Investigate some of your age-old work habits and routines. It may be time to replace these with more workable ones. For example, persisting with "sleep time" for all children in a preschool group as the year progresses can often cause more problems than benefits. Try a relaxation and visualization session instead.

WORKABLE SYSTEMS

Replace caffeine drinks, such as tea, coffee, and cola, with herbal teas during the day. For example, chamomile tea is now a widely accepted calming drink. Peppermint tea has cleansing and calming properties. Dandelion root is a good coffee substitute and is useful in the treatment of anxiety. Chai is a popular Indian drink and has calming, relaxing properties when used in one of its caffeine-free versions. Add honey or a slice of lemon to herbal teas to make them more appealing.

REPLACE CAFFEINATED BEVERAGES WITH HERBAL TEAS

Play quiet, relaxing music in the background in your work environment. Music can have a profound effect on our feelings of stress and anxiety. The ideal relaxation music has a slow tempo and rhythm: ambient, instrumental, and slow baroque pieces. Experiment with music that your colleagues

PLAY MUSIC

will enjoy and build on your collection of CDs or tapes over time. Children will especially enjoy hearing a variety of music during their day.

TAKE BREAKS Take short breaks during the day to breathe deeply, stretch, revive, and replenish. Stretching exercises at your office desk, a tai chi exercise, or a short walk will energize your body and lift your spirit.

REWARD YOURSELF Provide yourself with small treats and rewards occasionally. For example, meet a friend in a café after completing a big work assignment, or schedule an aromatherapy massage once a month as a treat.

SEPARATE WORK FROM HOME LIFE AND PERSONAL TIME When you are working, work; when you are relaxing, relax. Often the lines are blurred between work and relaxation time. Sometimes we waste valuable work time by daydreaming and wishing we were relaxing in the outdoors. This results in unfinished tasks and loss of productive time. Conversely, some people never "turn off," even when they think they are relaxing. For example, worrying about a deadline during a brisk walk on the weekend will defeat the purpose of this relaxation pursuit. Try to create a positive balance between work and relaxation in your life.

COMMUNICATE Communicate your needs to the people around you. Feelings of stress often arise when we fail to state our needs directly and assertively. If you require uninterrupted time during the day for important tasks, you need to tell those around you. Try to negotiate a balance at work so that everyone's needs are acknowledged.

MAKE TECHNOLOGY WORK FOR YOU In these days of labor-saving devices such as telephones, faxes, cellular phones, and computers, we are often bombarded with technological overload. Make your telephone work for you by installing an answering machine or voice mail so that your day is not consumed in answering calls. Don't allow new technology to make you accessible to everyone all the time, but use technology to protect your time and space while allowing people to leave you messages as needed.

Develop an overriding philosophy in your life. Regard relaxation as a way of being rather than something that we do to ourselves and others. *It is a way of transforming stress and anxiety in life through a relaxed, gentle, calm, life-enhancing approach to living.* Incorporating the above holistic suggestions on a daily basis will help you to be more relaxed in all areas of your life. The aim is to implement relaxation practices in your life's philosophy and enjoy participating in these each day. This will help you develop the skills and self-understanding to deal with stressful situations when they arise. By developing positive health habits and practicing relaxation strategies, teachers are simultaneously modeling techniques for children and getting in touch with their feelings and reducing their own stress. As Greenman (2002) says: "Adults largely set the emotional landscape for children. Children depend on us to be strong and solid, to know what is happening and guide them through the shoals of troubled waters" (p. 14).

Getting Started

When teachers are introducing relaxation techniques to children, careful planning and preparation are needed. This chapter will guide you through the planning process and help you think about your relaxation program so that the beginning can be smooth and productive for you and your students. We'll discuss the following topics:

- ❖ Setting the foundation
- ❖ Defining the teacher's role
- ❖ Structuring the session
- ❖ Managing children's behavior
- ❖ Helping parents use relaxation at home

Ideally, a tai chi and relaxation session takes place for at least twenty minutes per day. Tai chi and relaxation will not appeal to everyone—adults and children alike. Therefore, like any activity, it is worth giving it a try and experiencing its benefits—there is nothing to lose by doing this. If children do not feel comfortable in undertaking any of these exercises, allow them to sit and watch or engage in an alternative activity while other children are participating in it.

Providing a strong foundation for setting up a relaxation session involves some important decisions for teachers. It's helpful to collaborate with other

SETTING THE FOUNDATION

adults in the space and also to ask the children for their input as you consider how to make space and time in your program for relaxation. The following are the main things you will be thinking about:

- Provide a quiet space
- Set the scene
- Use soothing music
- Respect the relaxation space
- Provide consistent routines and rituals for relaxation time

Provide a quiet place   The space needs to be intimate and calming, yet big enough for all participants to do the tai chi movements without touching others and for them to have their own space when they lie on the floor without disturbing one another or encroaching upon one another's space. The room or space you use for relaxation should be large enough for all children to lie on the floor without touching each other. The area needs to be clean, warm, carpeted, away from noise and traffic areas, and, if possible, have soft lighting, such as lamps.

Set the scene   The children can help you dress the room or area used for relaxation as part of their daily activities. For example, have posters of scenes from nature on the walls. Decorate the area with potted plants, flowers, and mobiles. Have a relaxation or awareness book corner and provide cushions for when individuals or small groups of children want to spend time in the area apart from designated relaxation sessions. A fish tank, candles, soft, exotic draping materials, and relaxing music all add to the ambience of your special relaxation space. Once you have been through a few relaxation sessions, you can add children's drawings of their visualizations. Aesthetics are important to a relaxing experience.

Use soothing music   There are some excellent compact discs and tapes available for relaxation with adults and children. Browse your local teachers' supply or music shop and seek out ambient music with rainforest, beach, bird, dolphin, or other relaxing themes. Play this music at other times of the day to signal the need for calm, quiet activity. It will help the children become more relaxed and at ease during the day.

Start with an attitude of reverence and respect for the relaxation space you and the children have created together. Have the children remove their shoes but keep their socks on. No special clothing is required, but, in winter, children might need a small mat to lie on and a blanket to cover them while they are doing their relaxation.

Respect the relaxation space

One key to successful relaxation sessions with children is the development of a routine. Choose a relaxation time and stick to it each day. Ensure that the children know what they need to do on entering and leaving the space. If not, provide a gentle reminder of your expectations. Do not proceed with the tai chi or relaxation exercises unless the children are ready to listen.

Provide consistent routines and rituals for relaxation time

A greeting and good-bye ritual is useful and engages the children's interest. One derived from tai chi practice is to make a fist with your right hand. This is your "sun." Then place your left hand around your fist. This is your "moon." Raise your sun/moon to your forehead and bow slightly. This is a ritual of respect and reverence.

 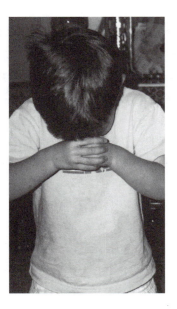

DEFINING THE TEACHER'S ROLE

The teacher's role is one of leader and participant. It is helpful if other available adults share relaxation time as well (student teachers, assistants, parents, even invite the director or school principal to join in!). You are the model and guide for the children. They will reflect your attitudes to the relaxation sessions. Too many times I have seen staff stand on the sidelines (some even chatting away), fully expecting the children to learn to relax but giving no thought to their own tense and off-putting behavior. We are fortunate in centers and schools as we can actually put our stress management ideas into practice on a daily basis with our children. It is not so easy if we work in a shop or a bank! It is vitally important for you to share your responses to the tai chi exercises and to talk about your feelings and experiences after the relaxation sessions with the children, as well as expecting them to listen and share. It is *your* attitude and approach to all aspects of relaxation that will make or break the program. The following are some ways you can model a relaxed attitude for the children:

- Use a calm and reassuring voice
- Give children frequent encouragement
- Accept whatever children say about their experience as true for them
- Share your own experience briefly

Use a calm and reassuring voice

The tone of your voice is important. Keep it firm but not overly loud. Speak naturally but evenly and slowly. Use expression and voice intonation to emphasize words. You may need to repeat key words or phrases a couple of times. Remember—slow . . . clear . . . calm.

Give children frequent encouragement

Children need affirmation and encouragement throughout the relaxation session. Ensure that you genuinely and warmly provide children with positive and reassuring feedback throughout the exercises, the progressive relaxation and visualization time, and in the follow-up group discussion.

We all respond to and experience relaxation in different ways. Some people actually "see" the images being described to them, while others have vague images or impressions of the spoken words. Other people can actually sense, smell, and hear the things that are being described. Others cannot visualize at all but enjoy the light and the sensations they feel when they are relaxing. No two children will have exactly the same experience in relaxation sessions. It is important for the teacher to accept and affirm the offerings and responses children make to the relaxation techniques. If any silliness arises, simply outline your expectations again and redirect the children's attention to a key word or to a comment offered by another child. You will find that relaxation time becomes cherished by the children and that any off-putting behavior quickly diminishes.

Accept whatever children say about their experience as true for them

Much of what you do in relaxation may be new for some children. Sharing feelings always involves risk-taking for children. Your willingness to share with children shows them that you are also willing to take that risk, and demonstrates how to do it. This makes a new task easier.

Share your own experience briefly

I first began introducing relaxation techniques when I was a young teacher with a class comprised of twelve- to sixteen-year-old children with emotional and behavior disabilities. All of the children in my class experienced severe learning problems. It took a lot of courage and persistence to embark on a relaxation program. Preparing the children beforehand was vital. A short discussion about the stresses the children were experiencing on the day and the resultant outcomes led to exploring suggestions for dealing with these stresses. I explained that I was learning tai chi, yoga, and meditation after school. I asked if they would like to try some of these techniques in class time. All but one child agree to give it a try. The one dissenter chose to watch us on some days and on other days was asked to sit with our principal for the duration of the session.

Anything new will create an anticipatory buzz in the room, so the expectations for the relaxation space need to be emphasized before starting. Chatter and giggles were features of our early tai chi sessions. In a short time (a few days of regular practice), these behaviors diminished. The usual behavioral difficulties arose when children touched or bumped each other, including name-calling, teasing, threats, and retaliating with a slap or a punch. I found that I needed to reinforce the importance of each child finding his or her own space and respecting the space of others.

When progressive relaxation and visualization were introduced, it took some time before the children felt comfortable about closing their eyes. I did not make this a requirement, but the children soon learned that they had a much more relaxing and meaningful experience if they tried to keep their eyes closed. Again, the temptation to nudge and poke their neighbor lying beside them was often irresistible; this often resulted in verbal fights, insults, or uncontrollable giggling. Again, I found it necessary to keep a calm tone of voice and slowly remind the children of my expectations for them during relaxation. If any one child became too noisy or disruptive, I invited him or her to sit near me or at the side of the relaxation space and watch without disturbing the enjoyment and participation of the others. Curiosity got the better of our nonparticipant and he began to join in. This child had extreme emotional disabilities and had suffered ongoing abuse throughout his life, so his progress was regularly punctuated with setbacks. The other children were well used to his outbursts and were remarkably accepting on the occasions he swore at me, told me relaxation was "stupid," and threw things around the room. At the onset of these inappropriate behaviors, he was told to leave the room with my teacher's aide and go to the principal, who was kind enough to talk to him calmly and sit with him until he was ready to join us after the relaxation session.

It took about seven months before this child was able to participate in relaxation sessions consistently and appropriately. At other times, if he or one of the other children became restless during visualization, I would sit beside them and gently stroke their back to help "ground" and settle them. I always asked the children if it was okay before doing this. Policies and procedures around safe touch for children need to be addressed as part of the preplanning for relaxation sessions.

One of the biggest risks the children faced was to join in with the post-relaxation discussion time. This is a stretch for anyone, but especially threatening for children with such severe emotional disabilities and shattered self-esteem. The children were encouraged to listen to and be accepting of their classmates' responses to tai chi and relaxation.

I found it important to share my feelings and experiences with the children—to act as a model for them and to reinforce the fact that everyone has worries, fears, and uncertainties. I was also able to model positive responses to the visualization experience by offering the images I "saw" and words that described my feelings of relaxation and calm. My teacher's aide also joined in and shared her experiences as well. At first, the children would copy the responses of each other because it was the first thing that came to mind, or they were unsure that what they saw was "right." Once a climate of safety, acceptance, and openness was developed, the mimicking behavior stopped and children began to enjoy sharing their own stories and responses.

The child who wouldn't participate at the beginning became one of our biggest relaxation fans and made sure that he reminded me to include a relaxation session each day. He occasionally reprimanded other children for being silly during our sessions (an extreme case of "the pot calling the kettle black," I think!). By the end of the year, he was performing a set of chi gong movements without any teacher help and participating in visualization journeys that lasted over thirty minutes. He contributed to relaxation session discussion more readily than in other curriculum areas. He also experienced special satisfaction from drawing and writing about his relaxation experiences. I believe that these sessions became very cathartic for him and the other children.

I decided that if, as a young teacher, I could experience the above level of success with children who had such serious emotional disabilities and had experienced such extreme abuse, then the task of introducing relaxation sessions to regular schools would be less challenging.

The above behaviors are extremes and are not likely to occur in early childhood settings. I tell you this long story only to assure you that no matter how difficult you may find the children with whom you work, relaxation can help them and you to have better days together.

Teachers know their children well and should plan relaxation sessions accordingly. This involves placing potentially troublesome children beside you or another adult (another staff member, parent helper, or student) and strategically placing children who are likely to disturb one another on opposite sides of the space. Keep to your relaxation rules or expectations consistently; for example, "When the music starts, all talking needs to stop," and so on.

STRUCTURING THE SESSION

When you start doing relaxation sessions with your children, it's helpful to have an outline to follow. As you become more comfortable and familiar with using relaxation exercises in your setting, you will begin to structure your relaxation sessions around the needs of your children each day. The following structure is what I use for my relaxation sessions; I encourage you to use this until you feel completely comfortable with the process, and then adapt it as necessary for your class.

- ❖ Beginning circle
- ❖ Tai chi exercises
- ❖ Progressive relaxation and visualization
- ❖ A sharing circle

Beginning circle

Have the children enter the space and form a circle. Use the tai chi greeting (sun and moon) and bow. Then ask the children to sit on the floor and briefly explain what they will be doing. Just provide a sentence or two by way of introduction. For example, you might say, "Today we will be practicing the tai chi exercises we learned yesterday. Can anyone remember the names of any of the movements? When we have completed our tai chi exercises we will be lying down on the floor to enjoy some relaxation and visualization time. Would anyone like to say or ask anything about relaxation before we start?" Don't take longer than a minute or two to do this. The aim is to begin the practice as quickly as possible before the children become restless.

Ask the children to spend a few seconds with their eyes closed, focusing on their breathing in order to "center" the group. A candle or a float bowl with flowers helps set the scene, and children who don't want to close their eyes can focus on this instead. Don't spend more than five minutes on this part of the session. It paves the way for what follows.

Have the children stand up and quietly find their own space, facing you. Begin the tai chi exercises slowly. Follow the instructions for teaching the tai chi exercises as they are presented in chapter 4. In your first sessions, introduce two or three exercises only. Remember that each exercise needs to be repeated several times for the children to gain benefit from the movements. Monitor your children's responses and teach the tai chi movements accordingly. If you feel they can only manage one or two exercises to start with, that is fine. Conversely, some children may indicate (by their participation and motivation to continue) that they are able to undertake more of the exercises.

Gently build up the number of exercises you teach each session. There are no strict guidelines here. The philosophy of tai chi is that it should flow naturally and the children should enjoy the exercises as they play out the movements. These exercises have been simplified for children. When teaching the exercises to children it is important to maintain a balance between ensuring that the movements are done as closely as possible to the instructions but not being too rigid in your expectations—allow a little improvisation in the early weeks.

Don't be too laissez-faire about the way the children perform the movements, however. If the children are allowed to change the exercises to the point where they become unrecognizable, there is no point teaching this method of movement and relaxation.

Talk to the children as you progress through the exercises and encourage them as you would with any other new skill to be learned. Provide realistic feedback and use vicarious reinforcement as a way of ensuring that the

children are doing the exercises correctly. Make the tai chi exercises fun and enjoyable and praise them for their successes in learning each one. For example, give them feedback such as, "You are all doing very well. I like the way you are following my movements carefully"; "Liyann is breathing in and out when I tell her to"; and "Look at how Farroud is doing 'Holding Up the Sky.' See if you can make your arms like his."

Ensure, as far as possible, that the children are breathing in accordance with the directions provided. Don't allow overexaggeration of the movements (for example, children trying to race ahead or to reach farther than everyone else). If you need to stop the tai chi session, have the children return to the Horse Riding Stance, and take a few breaths together. Reinforce your expectations of the group and begin again. If you find that on some days it all becomes too much, then move on to the progressive relaxation and visualization parts of the session. Don't expect perfection from the children. Some days they may be feeling too hot, tired, restless, excited, and so on to do all the exercises you planned. Just as with any other activity you present, be prepared to be flexible in your delivery of tai chi and relaxation sessions.

A typical tai chi segment of the relaxation session would take the following form:

1. Greeting (bow)
2. Warm-up exercises
3. Tai chi movements
4. Closing ritual (bow, and so on)

Begin with short sessions (about five to ten minutes) and gradually increase the time up to twenty minutes for three- to six-year-olds and longer (thirty minutes or more) for older children. Gauge the children's energy levels and responses in each tai chi lesson and time it accordingly.

Progressive relaxation and visualization When you are done with the tai chi exercises, ask the children to lie down on the carpet on their backs, with their legs and arms relaxed and their eyes closed. (This can be threatening for some children, so gently encourage them to shut their eyes a little at a time and gradually lengthen the time the eyes are closed.) Ask them to relax one body part at a time, until they have paid attention to and relaxed their entire bodies. For example, say something like, "Now, relax your toes. Wiggle them around a little and then just let them go limp. Let your feet relax; let them get soft and loose. Let your legs relax. You can feel them getting soft, just as if they were melting; they're getting so relaxed . . ." and so on. There is a sample script for this kind of progressive relaxation exercise in chapter 5.

When all body parts have been relaxed, begin reading a visualization script (see chapter 5).

You will quickly develop your own style and rhythm for this and will not be reliant on actually reading it for more than a couple of weeks. Read slowly, using a calm and gentle voice that is just loud enough for all the children to hear. Include silent spaces within the script to allow for deeper relaxation where appropriate for your children's needs. A visualization script can take five minutes (if you shorten the script), or up to thirty minutes (if you expand on the script or include numerous long pauses). Again, take your signals from the children as you observe their responses and levels of participation. It is always best to start with short sessions (perhaps five or ten minutes) and work your way gradually toward longer sessions.

Always bring children out of a visualization/relaxation exercise slowly and respectfully. Do not ask them to open their eyes and stand up too quickly. The children need to reorient and "earth" themselves. If children are a little slow or tired after relaxation, do a couple of standing stretches or waist swings to reenergize them.

If your center or school does not use visualization, develop your own ways of providing rest and replenishment for young children after tai chi. Taking part in a visualization exercise is simply using the imagination to produce images (or pictures, feelings, and so on) that bring about a relaxation response. If you prefer to skip the visualization section of the relaxation time, you may like to substitute it with one or more of the following:

- ❧ Ask the children to lie down on the floor in their own space and listen to a piece of relaxation music (see references for details).
- ❧ Take the children outside and have them lie on the grass and watch the clouds float by or gaze into the tops of the trees.

- Ask the children to lie down in their quiet space/corner and read them a favorite book with a relaxing theme (steer away from stories that will excite or spook children—this will defeat the purpose of this special time) or even a fable, fairy tale, myth, or Bible story if appropriate. You can also have the children help you write their own quiet-time stories.
- Ask the children to lie down on the floor and dim the lights. Have them gaze up toward the ceiling at glow-in-the-dark stars and moons you have placed on the ceiling.
- Sitting in a circle, spend some time quietly watching a flickering candle; a flower floating in a bowl; some fish swimming in a large bowl; or a fountain consisting of a water bowl, some stones, and a small pump (readily available from department stores).

Sharing circle Have the children sit in a circle and hold hands, and feel the magic of the relaxation and energy they have created. A trick that children love is to rub their hands together and hold them up in the air to "catch the magic" in the room. Do this exercise three or four times, and tell them to stroke their tingling hands over their faces, arms, legs, and so on.

Now share a few responses and reactions to the relaxation session. Some children will want to talk about their tai chi, some will want to talk about their visualization journey, and some will not want to share their experiences at all.

Make a point of asking each child how they are and what their experiences were like. This part of the session can be followed up by painting, drawing, modeling, patterning, or creative movement activities. For example, if children have done a visualization on "A Walk in the Rainforest," they may want to paint or draw what they felt, saw, heard, smelled, and so on. See chapter 6 for more information about using creative work to follow up a tai chi/relaxation session.

It is not the purpose of this book to outline a range of methods for managing the inappropriate and at times troubling behavior of children. There is a wealth of texts on this subject. However, I strongly believe that the incorporation of an "ecology of relaxation" into early childhood centers and schools, as well as into children's homes, will serve as a preventative measure against many discipline problems highlighted by educators and parents alike.

Behavior problems should not arise if you talk to the children about what you will all be doing in the relaxation area. Explain why you are

MANAGING CHILDREN'S BEHAVIOR

doing tai chi and relaxation sessions and how it can help. Set up expectations for this area just as you would in any other activity. For example, stress the need to listen and pay attention, not to touch others, and to lie still during relaxations. Some young children enjoy holding a teddy bear ("relaxation bear") while they are lying down for progressive relaxation time. Stroking the bear can be soothing and calming. If children become restless, do a stretch (hands above heads, breathe in—bend down, touch the floor, breathe out) and then remind them of your expectations.

The relaxation techniques will become a treasured part of the children's days once they become used to the routine. When relaxation is first introduced to the children you may need to remind them to stay as quiet as possible, to keep their hands to themselves, listen carefully, and avoid interrupting another child's enjoyment of the session. Any minor problems will disappear once you find your own way to conduct these sessions. The following are a few examples of the small issues I have experienced in my classes with preschoolers:

❖ Once, two young girls (three years old) began a high-pitched squeal as they first began to do the tai chi movements. I am still not sure why they did this—they were enjoying the movements and were participating well. Perhaps they were squeals of delight and anticipation? I responded with an I-message: "When girls squeal while doing tai chi, I feel sad that the other children won't hear what I'm saying. Let's all do the exercises quietly." It worked immediately and the raucous squeals stopped.

- Some young boys (three- or four-year-olds) tried to turn the exercises into "martial arts" kicking and fighting movements. I might have avoided this in the first place by explaining from the beginning that we do not learn tai chi to hurt others but to help our bodies feel relaxed and calm. (Remember that the time you put into preparing the children for a tai chi/relaxation program is well worth it and can eliminate some issues from the start.) However, in this case I said something like, "When children don't follow the exercises along with me, I am worried someone will get hurt. Watch me carefully and do the movements just as I do them." If this doesn't work, you might also ask the child to sit down and watch the others until they feel ready to join in again. Remember that this "sitting down" time need only be a minute or two. The aim is to have the children *do* the exercises, not sit on the sidelines. It is often the children who try to act out that most need the benefits of tai chi.

- The children will quickly find favorites among the tai chi exercises. On a couple of occasions, I have had preschool children complain because they wanted to do their movement first. I usually reassured them that their favorite exercise will be done soon and that it was important for them to come back to their breathing and focus on the current exercise.

- It is often said that wisdom comes from the mouths of babes. One example of a time when I did *not* have to intervene was when a four-year-old boy reprimanded two of his classmates (both boys), saying: "You can't breathe in and out and talk too, so you are messing up your tai chi." I smiled to myself.

It is important for teachers to communicate with parents throughout the planning and implementation stages of the relaxation program. This two-way communication will lead to shared ideas, resources, and experiences. In this way, parents and teachers can work collaboratively on tailoring the relaxation program to suit the children's needs. The success of a school

HELPING PARENTS USE RELAXATION TECHNIQUES AT HOME

relaxation program can be enhanced when it is supported and used by parents at home (and vice versa).

Parents want what is best for their children, but often need guidance and support from teachers when trying different strategies. Parents often ask for help and ideas when they want their children to accomplish the following:

- Learn to slow down
- Develop concentration
- Fall asleep easily
- Experience contentment
- Connect with their inner selves

Teachers can use the handouts in the appendix to help parents who are interested to embark on relaxation time at home. Many of these ideas are similar to earlier suggestions provided for setting up a school relaxation program. Parents can adapt these ideas to suit their children's needs.

CHAPTER 4

Gentle Tai Chi Exercises

Relaxation strategies are a form of simple meditation for children (tai chi is often called moving meditation, and breathing and stillness in progressive relaxation and visualization are hallmarks of meditation practice). However, I do not refer to the relaxation techniques presented in this book as meditation for children, because I believe the word "meditation" conjures up images of adults sitting cross-legged for extended periods while trying to empty their minds to reach a state of nirvana. While I am exaggerating here, I want to emphasise that relaxation techniques for children can be simple, easy, fun, and, most important, everyday techniques that they participate in from a young age.

WARM-UP EXERCISES

As with other forms of exercise, it is important to warm up the muscles, ligaments, and joints of the body in preparation for tai chi movements. This can be done by performing simple limbering and stretching movements with the children. These warm-ups are not prescriptive and you can include any favorites you already use with your children.

These exercises can be modified for use with children with mobility problems and other physical disabilities.

Cleansing breath

1. Have the children find their own space and stand with their feet at about shoulder width apart.

2. Bend knees slightly and sink down a little.

3. Ask the children to breathe in and stretch their arms up over their heads (see A below).

4. Next, as the children breathe out, ask them to bend forward, trying to bring their hands down to touch their feet—without bending the knees too much (see B below). Return to the position in number 1.

5. Repeat this exercise a few times.

A. *Stretch arms up.*

B. *Touch feet.*

1. Ask the children to stand with their feet shoulder width apart and hold their arms bent at shoulder height with palms facing outward (see A below).

2. Without moving the body, push the palms out to the side, as if pushing against a wall (see B below).

3. Return to the position in A.

4. Repeat this exercise several times, adding variations if you wish (for example, hands reaching forward, and so on).

A. *Stand with palms facing outward.*

B. *Push palms out.*

Waist swings

1. Ask the children to stand with their feet shoulder width apart, holding their arms stretched out to their sides at waist height with palms down, breathing in (see A below).

2. Rotate the body around to the right side, breathe out, and face the back wall, keeping the arms out to the side and the feet "glued" to the floor (see B below).

3. Now swing slowly around through the front (breathe in) and around to the left side.

4. Look around to the back wall, breathing out as you turn your body.

5. Repeat this exercise several times.

A. *Stand with palms down.*

B. *Rotate to the right without moving feet.*

Tai Chi Ch'uan (often referred to as simply "tai chi") is an ancient form of Chinese exercise and soft martial art dating back hundreds of years.

Tai chi exercises are beneficial for the mind, body, and spirit for children and adults alike. The slow movements accompanied with rhythmical breathing enhance health, coordination, and flexibility. The "moving meditation" principles of tai chi create feelings of peace, harmony, calm, quiet, and happiness in children. Tai chi also promotes good posture, muscle tone, and suppleness.

Tai chi brings the body back into its natural balance. In urban Western society, physical exercise is no longer a part of everyday life for children (or adults!). While other forms of exercise (gymnastics, aerobics) can be useful, they often do not work on the joints, nor do they integrate the mind, body, and spirit. Growing bodies require lots of movement opportunities to help them develop. Traditional exercises and sports can be helpful for many children; however, inappropriate exercise and too much competitive sport can be damaging. It is vital, therefore, to introduce children to gentle, noninvasive exercise in order to develop a healthy, balanced lifestyle before negative habits set in.

I have developed the following sequence of tai chi movements for children, to be undertaken before progressive relaxation and visualization exercises. I believe that before the mind can relax, the body must learn to relax. Tai chi gently prepares the body and the mind to become still, calm, and relaxed.

Children often tell me how much they enjoy hearing the names of the different movements, and some children have even created their own names for them.

Repeat each movement one to eight times, depending on the age of the children and the stage through which they are progressing with their tai chi. Begin by introducing only two or three movements and gradually build up to the whole set of movements over time. Once you have learned most or all of the movements in the book, choose four to six movements to practice each session. Over time, as you develop more proficiency in tai chi, you may want to consult a reference or take a tai chi course, and adapt other tai chi poses to work with young children.

MOVEMENT 1

Raising the arms
(wu chi 1)

1. Place your feet shoulder width apart.

2. Slightly bend your knees and sink down a little. This is commonly known as the "Horse Riding Stance." Breathe in and out naturally. Keep your spine straight. It is important to commit this movement to memory as most tai chi movements start from this stance (see A below).

3. Stand with your feet almost parallel.

4. Raise both your arms to shoulder height in front of you, shoulder width apart with palms facing down. Breathe in as you do this and imagine your arms floating up to shoulder height like balloons (see B below).

5. Slowly move your palms down until your hands are by your sides again (see C below). Breathe out as you do this.

6. Slightly bend your knees as you lower your arms.

7. Repeat this movement a few times.

A. *Preparing for wu chi in the Horse Riding Stance.*

B. *Imagine your arms floating up to shoulder height like balloons.*

C. *Slowly move your arms down toward your sides.*

1. Begin in the Horse Riding Stance. Breathe naturally. Hold a comfortable posture.

2. Raise both arms to shoulder height in front of you with palms facing down, breathing in as you do this.

3. As in wu chi, imagine your arms floating up like balloons (see A below).

4. As you breathe out, extend your arms out to the sides at shoulder height, palms facing forward (see B below).

5. Breathe in and return to the position illustrated in A.

6. Return to the Horse Riding Stance.

7. Repeat this movement a few times.

MOVEMENT 2

Expanding the heart (wu chi 2)

A. *As you breathe out, begin to extend your arms to the sides.*

B. *Fully extend your arms outward as you breathe out.*

MOVEMENT 3

Holding up the sky

1. Begin in the Horse Riding Stance (see A below).
2. Link fingers with palms facing upward.
3. Inhaling, draw the palms slowly upward while rising onto the balls of the feet (see B below).
4. Turn the palms over when they reach chest height (see C below).
5. Still inhaling, continue to press the palms upward while fully stretching the body toward the sky.
6. Follow the hands with your gaze (see D and E below).
7. Hold the inhalation for about three counts and then slowly exhale, gradually reversing the order of the movements.
8. Remember to turn the palms back over at chest height.
9. Complete the movement and exhalation at the beginning posture (back to A).

A. *Begin in the Horse Riding Stance.*

B. *Link your fingers, with the palms facing upward.*

C. *Draw the palms slowly up to chest height.*

D. *Turn the palms outward as you continue to raise your arms.*

E. *Extend the linked hands above your head.*

MOVEMENT 4

Turning the waist and pushing the palm

1. Begin in the Horse Riding Stance (see A below).
2. Keeping the feet firmly on the ground, begin to turn the waist 45 degrees to the left as you inhale.
3. At the same time, raise your right arm with palm facing up, and then bring your right hand, palm facing left, across your body at chest height.
4. As you exhale, push to the back with your right palm as you turn farther around to the left.
5. Keep your left palm turned over beside you and press it down beside your left thigh (see B below).
6. Return to the Horse Riding Stance.
7. Repeat the movement.
8. Inhale, this time turning the body 45 degrees to the right and raising your left arm with palm facing up. Then push out around and behind you with the left palm as you exhale (see C below).
9. Return to the Horse Riding Stance.
10. Repeat the movement to alternate sides several times.

A. *Begin in the Horse Riding Stance.*

B. *Exhale as you push your right hand out behind you, turning your body to the left.*

C. *Repeat using the left hand and turning your body to the right.*

1. Begin in the Horse Riding Stance (see A below).

2. Raise your hands in front of your body and take them over your head.

3. Shift body weight to the right side.

4. Bend the right knee and at the same time curve the right palm over the head so that it faces the top of your head, then inhale. The elbow is relaxed in a gentle curve.

5. Simultaneously, lower the left arm to shoulder height on the left side of the body, turning the body slightly to the left to look out at the left palm. Exhale (see B below).

6. Reverse arms by repeating the movements to the other side.

7. Raise the left hand up over the head so the palm faces the top of the head.

8. Weight is on the left leg with the left knee bent. Inhale.

9. Simultaneously, lower right arm to shoulder height on the right side of the body.

10. Palm up, turn the body to the right, look at right palm. Exhale (see C below).

11. Repeat movement on alternating sides several times.

A. *Begin in the Horse Riding Stance, then raise your arms above your head.*

B. *Curve the right palm over your head and lower your left arm out to the side.*

C. *Change arms. Repeat the movement by curving the left arm over your head and lowering your right arm out to the side.*

MOVEMENT 6

Punching in a Horse Riding Stance

This is a martial arts movement and it should be stressed to the children that we never use our fists (or any part of our bodies) to hurt another person. This movement can help children to relieve stress. Suggest to the children that they imagine they are punching away any anger, worry, tiredness, silliness, or wriggles as they do this movement. The preschoolers I worked with called this movement "Star Fists," as they liked to release the outward punch and extend their fingers out like stars.

1. Begin in the Horse Riding Stance.
2. Draw hands into fists, bend elbows, and raise the hands to the side of the waist, knuckles facing down. Inhale (see A below).
3. As you punch forward with the right fist, twist it over, so the knuckles face up at chest height. Exhale (see B below).
4. Draw the fist back down to the side of your waist, rotating the wrist to bring the knuckles back to the starting position (see A).
5. Repeat the movement using the left hand (see C below).
6. Repeat this movement several times.

A. *Draw hands into fists (knuckles down) and raise them to waist height.*

B. *Punch forward—slowly— with the right fist, turning the knuckles over as you do this.*

C. *Repeat the movement by drawing the right fist in and slowly punching outward— knuckles up—with the left hand.*

1. Begin in the Horse Riding Stance.
2. Inhale, crossing hands at wrists, palms up to chest height (see A below).
3. Exhale as you uncross your hands, raising them to the sides, palms down, at shoulder height (see B below).
4. Repeat this movement several times.

A. *Inhale, cross hands at wrists, moving your palms up to chest height.*

B. *Raise your arms to the sides, palms down, at shoulder height.*

MOVEMENT 8

Stepping and bouncing a ball

1. Begin in the Horse Riding Stance (see A below).
2. Inhale as you raise the right arm up to just above shoulder height, raising your right knee up at the same time.
3. Exhale as you lower your right arm and your right leg (see B below).
4. Repeat on the other side. Inhale as you raise your left arm to just above shoulder height and raise your left knee and left arm at the same time.
5. Exhale as you lower your left hand and left knee (see C below).
6. Repeat the movement several times, imagining that you are bouncing a large ball in front of you.

A. *Begin in the Horse Riding Stance and then start to bend your right leg, ready to raise it off the ground.*

B. *Inhale and raise your right arm and right knee at the same time (pretending you are bouncing a ball). Exhale.*

C. *Reverse the movement by raising the left arm and left knee slowly as you inhale. Exhale.*

1. Begin in the Horse Riding Stance.
2. Bring weight to your right side. Bend right knee over your right foot.
3. Inhale as you raise your right arm (palm down) out to shoulder height (see B below).
4. Exhale as you lower your right arm and come through the center to the Horse Riding Stance
5. Repeat with weight on left leg, left knee bent, raising left arm to shoulder height (see C below).
6. Repeat to both sides several times.

Spinning silken threads from the bottom of the ocean

A. *Begin in the Horse Riding Stance.*

B. *Bring your weight to your right side. Raise your right arm and bend your right knee over your toes.*

C. *Reverse the movement by raising your left arm and bending your left knee over your toes.*

MOVEMENT 10

Salute to the sun

1. Begin with feet nearly together.
2. Place hands in prayer position at chest height (see A below).
3. Raise hands up past face, release, and stretch hands above head, palms facing forward as you inhale (see B below).
4. Exhale as you bend your body slowly down to touch the floor with your fingertips.
5. Look down (lower head; see C below).
6. Slowly unfurl your body until you reach a standing position.
7. Place your hands back in prayer position.
8. Breathe in and out naturally for this part of the movement (see A below).
9. Repeat this movement several times.

A. *Place hands in prayer position at chest height. Your feet are nearly together.*

B. *Inhale as you stretch your arms above your head, palms facing forward.*

C. *Exhale and bend down slowly to touch the floor with your fingertips.*

1. Begin in the Horse Riding Stance. Breathe naturally. Hold a comfortable posture (see A below).

2. As you inhale, step forward with the left foot and extend both arms forward and upward to shoulder height, keeping the palms facing down. Bend your upper body slightly forward (see B below).

3. As you exhale, bring the arms down and allow the upper body to lean slightly backward (see C below), transferring your weight to the back foot. Then bring the arms up and shift forward again. The arms should move rhythmically as in a rowing movement.

4. Repeat these movements two to three times. Then return to the Horse Riding Stance.

5. Repeat on the opposite foot. As you breathe in, step forward with the right foot and follow with the breathing and the arm movements as described above. Repeat two to three times.

MOVEMENT 11

The rowing boat

A. *Begin in the Horse Riding Stance.*

B. *Step forward and extend arms.*

C. *Bring arms down and back, and lean back slightly.*

MOVEMENT 12

I'm tall—I'm short

1. Begin in the Horse Riding Stance. Breathe naturally. Hold a comfortable position (see A below).

2. Inhale and take a small step to the left. Exhale as you bend your knees to lower your body (to a half-squatting position). At the same time, slightly bend your elbows and lightly press the palms downward (see B below).

3. Return to the Horse Riding Stance.

4. Repeat the movement, this time stepping to the right. Then return to the Horse Riding Stance.

5. Repeat the entire exercise two to three times on each side.

6. Remember to keep your body relaxed when you bend your knees.

A. *Begin in the Horse Riding Stance.*

B. *Step to one side and bend knees.*

1. Begin in the Horse Riding Stance. Breathe naturally. Hold a comfortable posture (see A below).

2. As you inhale, step out with the left foot, keeping the heel down and the toes facing upward. At the same time, raise both hands to chest height, palms facing outward, turning your body slightly to the left-hand corner of the room (see B below).

3. Exhale as you move your body weight forward. At the same time, bend your left knee and extend the arms out to the front at shoulder height—palms still facing outward (see C below).

4. Inhale as you lower your arms and transfer your weight to the back (right) foot. Your left toes point upward as you rest on your left heel (see B).

5. Repeat the above movement two to three times with your left foot remaining forward.

6. Swap feet—placing your right foot forward—and repeat the entire exercise, this time with the body slightly facing the right-hand corner of the room.

I can push the waves

A. *Begin in the Horse Riding Stance.*

B. *Step out and raise hands.*

C. *Move forward, bending knee and pushing palms out.*

MOVEMENT 14

The peaceful dove opens its wings

1. Begin in the Horse Riding Stance. Breathe naturally. Hold a comfortable position (see A below).

2. As you exhale, step out with the left foot, slightly facing the left-hand corner of the room. Place your left foot flat on the floor, moving your body weight forward over your left knee. At the same time, raise your arms to shoulder height, palms facing each other (see B below).

3. Inhale as you transfer your weight back to your right foot, bending your right knee and almost straightening your left leg, resting on the left heel, toes pointing upward. Bring your arms out to the side to shoulder height—palms facing forward. Exhale (see C below).

4. Repeat on the left-hand side two to three times.

5. Return to the Horse Riding Stance.

6. Repeat the entire movement a few times, this time stepping out with the right foot, slightly facing the right-hand corner of the room.

A. *Begin in the Horse Riding Stance.*

B. *Step out, shift forward, and raise arms.*

C. *Shift back and open arms.*

1. Begin in the Horse Riding Stance. Breathe naturally. Hold a comfortable position (see A below).

2. Inhale as you place your hands on your hips and turn your body to the right side, keeping both feet flat on the floor. Bend over at the waist to the right-hand side, keeping your head up and your back fairly flat (see B below).

3. Exhale as you slowly rotate to the left-hand side in this "flat back" position. Complete the movement by raising the body up, remaining slightly turned toward the left-hand side, ready to start the movement again from the opposite side (see C below).

4. Repeat the movement, this time starting on the left-hand side.

5. Repeat the entire movement on each side two to three times.

Bend and stretch

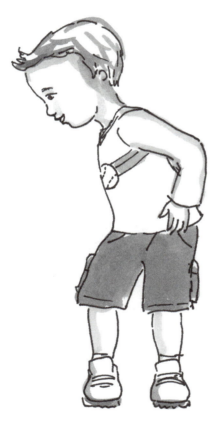

A. *Begin in the Horse Riding Stance.*

B. *Turn and bend, keeping back flat.*

C. *Rotate to the other side and raise torso up.*

MOVEMENT 16

Flying like a peaceful dove

1. Begin in the Horse Riding Stance. Breathe naturally. Hold a comfortable posture (see A below).

2. As you inhale, raise your body and lift the heels. At the same time, raise your arms out to the sides and up until they are above head height (see B below). (Remain on flat feet if rising up slightly on the toes is too difficult or balance becomes unsteady.)

3. Exhale as you sink down, lowering the heels to the floor and returning to the Horse Riding Stance. Palms may face the thighs in this position before starting the next repetition of the movement (see C below).

4. Repeat the entire movement several times (two to three times).

A. *Begin in the Horse Riding Stance.*

B. *Lift heels and raise arms.*

C. *Lower heels and bring arms to sides.*

1. Begin in the Horse Riding Stance. Breathe naturally, holding a comfortable position (see A below).

2. Inhale, point toes slightly outward for balance, and place hands on hips (see B below).

3. Exhale as you bend forward, trying not to curve the back too much. (You don't need to touch your toes.) Turn your head to face toward the left and your bottom to the right (see C below).

4. Return to the Horse Riding Stance and breathe in and out gently.

5. Repeat the movement, this time turning your head to face the right and your bottom to the left (see D below).

6. Repeat on each side two to three times.

MOVEMENT 17

Shaking the head and wagging the tail

A. *Begin in the Horse Riding Stance.*

B. *Place hands on hips.*

C. *Bend forward, turning head and bottom in opposite directions.*

D. *Bend forward again, reversing direction of twist.*

MOVEMENT 18

Reaching for the moon

1. Begin in the Horse Riding Stance. Breathe naturally. Hold a comfortable posture (see A below).

2. Inhale as you move your weight to the left, turning your body toward the left and raising your arms up to head height on your left-hand side (see B below).

3. Exhale as you lower your arms and face the front, returning to the Horse Riding Stance.

4. Repeat the movement, this time moving your weight to the right, turning your body to the right, and raising your arms up to head height on your right-hand side (see C below).

5. Repeat the entire movement several times (two to three times).

A. *Begin in the Horse Riding Stance.*

B. *Turn to one side and raise arms on that side of head.*

C. *Repeat to the other side.*

1. Begin in the Horse Riding Stance. Breathe naturally. Hold a comfort-able posture (see A below).

2. Inhale and then exhale as you raise your right hand over your head—palm facing upward (fingers facing inward if possible). At the same time, rest your left hand beside your left thigh—palm facing downward (see B below).

3. Repeat entire movement several times (two to three times).

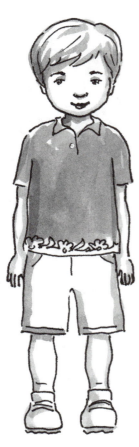

MOVEMENT 19

Plucking a star from the night sky

A. *Begin in the Horse Riding Stance.*

B. *Raise one hand and reach palm up.*

MOVEMENT 20

*Hold my magic
tai chi ball*

1. Begin in the Horse Riding Stance. Breathe naturally. Hold a comfortable position (see A below).

2. Inhale and pretend you are holding a small beach ball by placing your left hand on the "top" of your imaginary ball—palm down—and your right hand (supporting the ball) palm up "underneath" the ball (see B below), at chest height.

3. Exhale as you swap hand positions by placing your right hand on "top" of your imaginary ball (palm down) and your left hand (palm up) "underneath" the ball to support it (see C below).

4. Repeat the entire movement several times (two to three times).

5. Finish in the Horse Riding Stance.

A. *Begin in the Horse Riding Stance.*

B. *Hold a pretend ball with one palm up and the other down in front of you.*

C. *Reverse hand positions.*

CHAPTER 5

Relaxation and Visualization

After children do four to six tai chi exercises, it will be easier for them to move into progressive relaxation of their bodies, and then into a visualization exercise, if you choose to do one. (See chapter 3 for alternatives if your school or program prohibits the use of visualization.) Relaxation is a way of producing a quiet body and calm mind. Learning to relax involves becoming aware of the difference between muscle tension and muscle relaxation. Relaxing one's muscles also calms one's mind and emotions—it is not possible to feel agitated and relaxed at the same time.

WHAT IS PROGRESSIVE RELAXATION?

Progressive relaxation was developed by Jacobsen (1938; 1970) and is the most widely used relaxation procedure. It involves focusing the attention on body parts and using the breathing to help the muscles relax. Alternatively, the body parts or muscle groups can be progressively tensed and relaxed in turn, using the breath. When using relaxation with children, it is important to keep the process simple and use terminology that children can relate to.

A possible script for a progressive relaxation exercise

Here is a possible script for a progressive relaxation exercise. You might use the following script sequence as a guide to leading your children through progressive relaxation. Once you do this a few times, you will become comfortable with the process, and you won't need a script any longer. These are the kinds of directions I use in my relaxation sessions with children, though of course I don't use these exact words every day. The directions can be shortened or lengthened depending on the needs of the particular group. They are also suited to working with a single child.

The directions are spaced with paragraph breaks, indicating appropriate pauses. Encourage children's efforts periodically by comments like "You are doing very well," or "I'm pleased to see everyone lying so still and listening well." This is very important and reassuring for the children.

You will notice that the end of the script I have included here takes you right into one of the visualization scripts, which appear later in this chapter. If you are not using visualization, you can have the children lie quietly for a moment or two, feeling the relaxation in their bodies, and then gently prompt them to open their eyes. When they are ready, slowly get up, and move into whatever you have planned next, perhaps some kind of creative activity.

If you choose to, you may begin the relaxation session by playing soft, soothing music in the background.

"Feel your whole body resting on the floor. Try to allow your hands and feet to be very still. Now, with the help of your breathing, we are going to gradually let your body relax. Try to feel your breathing. Feel the flow of your breath entering your body and leaving it again. As you breathe out, let go . . . relax . . . allow this relaxed feeling to become stronger and stronger, deeper and deeper."

. . .

"Now feel that your very light, soft breathing is allowing you to relax more and more."

. . .

"Now try to feel your body parts. Feel your feet and toes. Can you feel your toenails? Breathe in and curl your toes under very tightly—this is tension—now let them unwind as you breathe out and feel your feet relaxing . . . feel the tension leave every part of your body. Relax your ankles, breathing in and out."

. . .

"Feel the lower part of your legs between your knees and your ankles. Can you feel the weight of your legs as they press against the floor?"

. . .

"As you breathe out, just let the lower part of your legs relax. Relax your knees. Breathe in and move your attention to the tops of your legs and see if you can feel those big muscles there. Let them relax . . . let them become soft and flowing as you breathe out. Feel the whole length of your legs very relaxed."

• • •

"Breathe in and relax your bottom . . . let your bottom feel as if it is sinking into the carpet . . . breathe out."

• • •

"Now feel right along your back . . . try to feel the part of your back that doesn't quite touch the floor . . . feel yourself stretching out taller as you lie there. Breathe in."

• • •

"Can you feel the very soft movement of your breathing in your back? Can you be so quiet inside yourself that you can feel the movement of each breath as it flows in and out of your back?"

• • •

"Now as you breathe out, allow your back to relax completely . . . sinking into the floor. Just let your back melt . . . really try to feel that lovely relaxed feeling coming into your back now. Feel your shoulders relax as you breathe in and out."

• • •

"Relax your arms, elbows, wrists, hands, and fingers as you slowly breathe in and out."

• • •

"Relax your head, your forehead, your eyes, your nose, and your mouth as you slowly and gently breathe in and out."

• • •

"You are all doing very well. Try to keep that relaxed feeling as you lie on your space on the floor . . . we are all now going on a journey in our imaginations."

Now turn to one of the visualization scripts on the following pages.

Visualization (or guided imagery) is a process used with young children whereby they are asked to lie down, take some relaxing breaths, close their eyes, and engage in an exercise led by their teacher or a parent. Through the process we create a story or scene in the children's imaginations. The visualization scripts—usually focusing on scenes from nature, imaginary friends,

WHAT IS VISUALIZATION?

animals, or symbols of relaxation—allow the children to participate in their imaginations or thoughts and with their feelings, in a nonthreatening way. At the end of the visualization process, the children are gently encouraged to bring their awareness back to the room and provision is made for follow-up discussion and expression in a variety of ways.

Visualization techniques continue naturally from the progressive relaxation techniques (Thomas 1994). It is important to provide a quiet time for children each day to help them learn to value quiet, peace, stillness, and reflection. It gives them time out from busy routines, overstimulation, noise, and a hurried life.

The visualization scripts included here are really just examples of the kinds of guided imagery I use with children. You may want to use these verbatim to begin with, but over time, as you grow accustomed to them, you will want to modify them to make them your own. You may even want to create scripts for imaginary journeys not represented here. As you do so, remember that the purpose of the visualization is for children to relax and connect more deeply with nature and their own inner spirit. The visualization is meant to be calming, not adventurous or exciting.

As with the relaxation script, read or say the visualization slowly and clearly, in a calm, soothing voice. The paragraph breaks indicate pauses where you may want to stop reading for a few moments to give children a chance to visualize their own journey.

"As you are lying in this place of peace and relaxation, I want you to come for a walk with me in your imagination. We are going to walk out of this room, through the playground, until you come to a beautiful forest path. As you begin to walk down your forest path, you start to hear the sounds of the forest—the birds calling and singing to each other, the rustling of the breeze through the trees, and some water flowing in the distance. As you walk down your forest path, notice the beautiful tall trees that lead you down. You know that you are very safe and secure while you are on this journey . . . we are all here to look after you."

· · ·

"You are not wearing any shoes and you can feel the dirt and leaves under your feet—and it feels good. Feel the gentle sun shining down on your face and feel the breeze whisper through your hair."

· · ·

"As you walk along, notice the beautiful flowers, ferns, and trees growing in the forest. What colors are there in your forest? Just notice them quietly to yourself."

· · ·

"Look up into the trees and watch the birds flying from branch to branch. What kinds of birds do you have in your forest?"

· · ·

"The sound of rushing water is becoming louder now as you walk farther down your forest path. You notice a beautiful forest pool being filled by a magical waterfall. Sit down on a rock beside your pool and feel the water trickling over your feet."

· · ·

"Sit beside your forest pool for a short while now."

· · ·

"What noises can you hear, sitting beside your pool?"

· · ·

"Look around at the beautiful plants, rocks, mosses, and ferns. Listen to the music and sit quietly by the pool for a while."

· · ·

"Now . . . we know it's time to leave our forest pool, but because this is a place that we have created in our imaginations, we can return here any time we wish."

· · ·

"But . . . for now . . . stand up from your rock and take one last look at this forest pool and begin walking back up your forest path."

.   .   .

"Make your way to the top of the path now and return back to our building, through the playground and the gardens, up to the door, and into our room."

.   .   .

"Now . . . still with your eyes closed, think about how you feel right now . . . are you relaxed and at peace? Think back to some of the lovely things you saw and felt in your rainforest."

.   .   .

"Now . . . gradually bring your mind back to our room and slowly bring your body out of the relaxation. Begin to wiggle your fingers and toes, gently move your body from side to side and slowly open your eyes. When you are ready, slowly sit up and look around the room and at everyone else who has been on this journey with you. How do you feel?"

.   .   .

"What a wonderful journey! You did very well!"

.   .   .

"We are now going to talk a little about our forest walk . . ."

"As you are lying here, beginning to feel more and more relaxed and at peace, I want you to imagine that we are walking out of the room and taking our path down to the beautiful rainforest that we have visited before. Look up at all of the beautiful tall trees as you pass."

.   .   .

"What smells and sounds are in your forest today? Can you hear the birds singing? What kinds of birds are in your forest? What colors are your birds? Can you smell the beautiful smells of the forest?"

.   .   .

"What trees and plants can you see today? Are there any flowers here?"

.   .   .

"It feels good to be in this place. This is your special place . . . a place to enjoy, a place to relax, and a place to dream. You are very safe with all of us around you and you are free to wander in your imagination."

.   .   .

"You now find that you have come to your magical forest pool. Sit down on your rock and look into the calm, clear water. Quietly look into the depths of the water."

.   .   .

"You notice, on the other side of the pool, that a beautiful creature has come out of the forest to take a drink. What kind of creature is it there . . . on the other side of the pool? It is very gentle and peaceful and it has lovely kind eyes. What is your creature? Is it a bird, another type of animal, or maybe a big teddy bear or some other magical character you have heard about in a storybook?"

.   .   .

"Say hello to the magical creature with your eyes. Greet it and send it your love. This animal has a very special message just for you. Listen carefully to the kind, secret message it has to give you."

.   .   .

"Spend a couple of minutes listening to the music, enjoying being happy with your new friend, and feeling relaxed and happy to be in this special place . . ."

.   .   .

"It is now time to leave this place for today, so say good-bye to your friend, knowing that you can come back here and spend time with it whenever you wish to."

.   .   .

"Begin walking up your forest path, taking in all the smells and sounds along the way. What do you notice as you walk back up the path? What do you see?"

. . .

"When you get back up to the top of your forest path, turn around and take one last look, and head quietly back to our building. Walk through the garden, through the door, into our room, and back to where you see yourself lying down."

. . .

"Before you open your eyes, think about your wonderful, new, imaginary friend and the walk you've taken today. How do you feel?"

. . .

"Now, gently begin to bring yourself out of the relaxation by wiggling your fingers and toes. Now, slowly open and close your hands and open and close your eyes. Gently sit up when you are ready. Take as much time as you need."

. . .

"We'll now spend some time talking about our magical forest friend . . ."

The forest is full of animals. (Girl aged six years)

"As you are lying here in this place of peace and relaxation, I want you to imagine that a beautiful big bird has come to our door and is asking you to come for a ride with it. What kind of bird has come to greet you? What does your bird look like? What colors are its feathers? What do its eyes look like? Is it an eagle, a dove, or some other magical bird that you have heard about in a story?"

.   .   .

"Imagine that you are walking out of the room, outside the door to where the bird is waiting, and you climb upon its back. You know that you are safe and secure while you go on this journey in your imagination."

.   .   .

"The bird takes off gently and flies over our building and above all the houses, schools, and shops. The bird flies over the park and we can see the trees, the flowers, and the playground as we pass."

.   .   .

"Our bird flies out over the waves . . . far out to sea until it arrives at a beautiful island in the middle of the ocean. The bird stops at the top of a big hill and lets you climb down, telling you that it will be back to collect you soon."

.   .   .

"As you wave the bird good-bye, you notice the ocean from way up high where you are standing. Look at the sparkling water, with the sun glimmering on the waves. As you look out to sea, you see some dolphins diving in and out of the water. How precious these beautiful creatures are. You also notice some seagulls flying through the sky. Enjoy just being here in this place of beauty and quiet and settle in to the happiness, exhilaration, and relaxation that comes from being near the ocean."

.   .   .

"As you are waiting for your bird to come back to collect you, think about all the things that make you such a special and unique person . . . the way you look, the people you love, your special friends, your faithful pets, and all the talents you have that make you the special person that you are. There is no one else in the world who is quite like you . . . there never has been and there never will be . . . you are very, very precious indeed."

.   .   .

"Now . . . your bird has arrived back on your island and you know that it is time to leave this place for today. Welcome the bird and climb onto its back . . . Now . . . enjoy the flight back to where we came from. Notice the waves, the rocks, the people on the beach. Feel the wind in your hair as the bird soars through the sky."

·   ·   ·

"The bird has now brought you back to our building and you carefully climb down. Whisper a good-bye to the bird and know that you can ride through the sky with it whenever you wish to do so. Watch the bird fly away and then return, in your mind, back to our room."

·   ·   ·

"Spend a short time, still with your eyes closed, thinking about your amazing flight with the bird. How do you feel? What was it like to go riding over the sea on a bird's back?"

·   ·   ·

"Gently begin to bring yourself out of relaxation now, by wiggling your fingers and your toes. Open and close your hands and your eyes. When you are ready, slowly begin to sit up and look around the room."

·   ·   ·

"We will now spend some time talking about our flight with our magical bird . . ."

"As you are lying here in this place of quiet, peace, and relaxation, I want you to come for a walk with me in your imagination. Leave our room and walk out the door, away from the building, and down the street. Gradually, you notice that the street is turning into a track. Imagine that your track leads you over the sand hills and down onto a beautiful beach."

.   .   .

"Walk along the sand by the water's edge and feel the water lapping at your feet. Feel the warm sun shining down on you and a gentle sea breeze on your face and hair."

.   .   .

"Can you see any birds overhead? Are they making any sounds? Can you see any dolphins jumping in and out of the waves in the distance?"

.   .   .

"As you are lying here, try to feel the waves in the ocean . . . feel the gentle movement of the waves as they flow up and down. Imagine your arms and legs and then your whole body floating up and down on the beautiful, clear blue water of the ocean."

.   .   .

"Enjoy the feeling of the waves . . . a floating, relaxing sensation . . . and the sun shining down on you from above. Notice the cool, relaxed feeling of being rocked by the water in a gentle, soft way."

.   .   .

"Now, let your imagination leave the ocean and just be aware of how your body is feeling right now, as you lie here on the floor. What sensations can you feel in your body? Does your body feel relaxed and calm?"

.   .   .

"Take a short time, with your eyes still closed, to remember your walk to the beach. What did you enjoy about being there? What did you see and hear while you were walking along the beach? How did your body feel when it was rocking like the waves?"

.   .   .

"Now, very gently begin to wiggle your fingers and toes as we start to come out of our relaxation. Gently open and close your hands and open and close your eyes. When you are ready, begin to sit up and look around the room, feeling refreshed and awake and ready to listen to what other people have to say about their relaxation."

.   .   .

"We'll now spend some time together talking about our walk by the sea . . ."

"As you are lying here in this place of peace and relaxation, I'd like you to imagine that you are walking away from our building and through the streets nearby. The streets gradually become open paddocks that lead to a path. We begin walking along this path, enjoying the scenery all around us . . . the trees, the green grass, the birds, the sun, and the gentle breeze waving in the branches of the trees."

.   .   .

"Begin to follow your path as it winds higher and higher up a big mountain. The walk up the mountain path is easy for you and you notice many beautiful rocks, flowers, and ferns along the way."

.   .   .

"When you arrive at the top of your mountain, you sit on a rock and take a rest. What do you see on your mountain? Are there lots of plants? . . . Do you see any animals, insects, or birds?"

.   .   .

"Stay seated on your rock on top of this wondrous mountain and take in the view. What does the sky look like today? What can you see?"

.   .   .

"As you are sitting in this peaceful place, remember what a special person you are. Really enjoy the feeling of being in this special place that you have created in your mind."

.   .   .

"Now stand up and begin walking back down your mountain path. Know that you can come back to sit on your rock on top of this mountain at any time, because this is a place that you have created in your imagination."

.   .   .

"Feel yourself walking back to our room and take note of how you feel right now. How do you feel after walking on this great mountain? Take a short time to enjoy this feeling of just being you . . . while you listen to the music in the background."

.   .   .

"Now very gently begin to wiggle your fingers and your toes as we bring our bodies and our minds out of our relaxation exercise for today. Gently move your body from side to side and have a little stretch. Open and close your hands and your eyes."

.   .   .

"Now, very gently, be sitting up and looking around the room, feeling refreshed and awake."

.   .   .

"We'll now spend a short time talking about our walk to the mountain . . ."

"As you are lying here on the floor, listening to your breathing and the music, you can feel yourself becoming more and more relaxed. Know that you are very safe and secure with us all as we do our relaxation and visualization exercises together. This is a time for you to let go, enjoy the quiet and the stillness—and just enjoy being you. You don't have to do anything, be anything, or say anything for the next little while."

.   .   .

"I want you to think of a picture that makes you feel relaxed. This can be a place (like our rainforest) or a very special thing (like a feather, a picture, a plant, a pet, or a smooth stone). Paint this picture in your mind as clearly as you can. Try to hold on to this picture in your mind while you are still experiencing the feeling of relaxation and peace."

.   .   .

"This picture will now become a symbol or picture of peace for you—whenever you think of this picture, you will feel the feelings of quiet, peace, and stillness around you. What is your special symbol of peace—is it a flower, a rainbow, a tree, or is it something quite different and special to you?"

.   .   .

"Now . . . spend a few more seconds with your peace symbol and then slowly begin to bring yourself out of your relaxation. Wiggle your fingers and your toes. Gently move your body from side to side and begin to stretch. In your own time, open and close your eyes gently, and slowly come out of your relaxation. When you sit up, you will be feeling refreshed and peaceful."

.   .   .

"We'll now spend some time talking about and drawing our peace symbols . . ."

"As you are lying in this place of peace and relaxation, I want you to imagine that we have left our room and that we have boarded an airplane. We are flying way up into the sky and as we hover over the clouds, we slowly begin to climb out of the plane. We step onto the huge bank of clouds outside our airplane."

.   .   .

"As far as you can see there are white, cotton-wool-like clouds immersed in bright light from the sun. The cloud nearest to you looks so comfortable that you decide to lie down on it."

.   .   .

"The feeling as you ride along on this cloud is one of being safe, secure, and very relaxed. The soft cloud supports and rocks you as you move through the sky. The feeling of floating way above the earth enables you to feel free, relaxed, and at peace. Enjoy this feeling of freedom and relaxation as you lie there listening to the music for a short time . . ."

.   .   .

"How does your body feel right now? Do you feel calm and relaxed? Are you ready to step back inside the airplane now?"

.   .   .

"Allow the plane to carry you back to earth and come back into our room where we are all lying in our relaxation position. Know that you can return to your relaxation cloud whenever you wish to because it is a scene that you have created in your imagination. Magical things happen when we dream, visualize, and imagine. We are able to do things that are not possible in real life."

.   .   .

"Now . . . begin to wiggle your fingers and your toes . . . and slowly come out of your relaxation. Move your body from side to side and slowly open your eyes. When you are ready, sit up and look around the room. Feel ready to share your thoughts with us and be ready to hear about the cloud journey that other people experienced . . ."

"As you are lying in this place of relaxation and quiet, I want you to gently listen to your breathing and the music. Feel your breathing and your body become soft and loose."

. . .

"As you lie there, I'd like you to imagine a beautiful white light flowing out of the top of your head and flowing down all around your body. Try to imagine yourself lying there surrounded by a pool of white, shining, sparkling soft light . . ."

. . .

"This is a light of love, peace, and protection just for you. Imagine the light is soothing, healing, and warming you . . ."

. . .

"Feel the radiance and beauty of this white light flowing all around you."

. . .

"Just as this light shines out peace and beauty, so do you. Think of yourself as the special person that you are and imagine your love and peace shining out into the world just as your light is doing."

. . .

"Now think of someone you love very much and send some of your loving thoughts to them. Imagine that person being surrounded by white light just as you are."

. . .

"Spend a short time enjoying the feeling of being relaxed, at peace, and immersed in this beautiful white light. Listen to the music and to your breathing."

. . .

"Now I want you to slowly come out of your relaxation, knowing that you can get back in touch with your white light whenever you wish because it is an image you have created in your mind."

. . .

"Now bring yourself out of your relaxation by gently moving your fingers and your toes. Slowly move your body from side to side. When you are ready, begin to sit up and look around the room, feeling refreshed and at peace."

"As you are lying here in this place of peace and relaxation, I want you to imagine your favorite garden. Is it in your backyard, or a park, or at a friend's house?"

.   .   .

"Come walking with me in the garden. As you leave our room, you begin to smell the flowers growing all around you. What kinds of flowers do you have growing in your garden? What colors are your flowers?"

.   .   .

"As you continue down your garden path, you come to a grass clearing where you find a seat beside a fish pond. Sit down on the seat and take a look into the pond. What do you see in the pond? Are there lilies, water plants, and maybe goldfish swimming around? Take in the feelings of peace and quiet as you sit beside this pond."

.   .   .

"Do any birds come to take a drink while you are there? Imagine that a small bird is sitting on your shoulder and whispering a message in your ear. What is the secret message that the bird is bringing you?"

.   .   .

"Spend a few minutes listening to the music and enjoying the sights, sounds, and smells of this garden."

.   .   .

"Now, with your eyes still closed, stand up from your garden seat and take one last look at your garden pond for today. You know that you can return here whenever you wish because this is a place that you have created in your imagination."

.   .   .

"Begin to walk back up your garden path now, noticing the many different flowers and trees that grow here. Slowly walk back into our room and prepare to come out of your relaxation."

.   .   .

"Gently begin to move your feet and hands and stretch your body. When you open your eyes and sit up, you will be feeling refreshed and ready to enjoy the rest of the day."

.   .   .

"We'll now spend a few minutes talking about what you saw and felt in your secret garden . . ."

My cloud has lots of colors. (Girl aged three and a half years)

"As you are lying here in your relaxation state, I want you to know that you are safe and protected while we go on this journey in our imaginations. Slowly leave our room and walk through the door outside and into the garden. Follow the garden path until you come to a big, green paddock that surrounds a beautiful lake. There are reeds growing around the lake and the water is clear, blue, and sparkling."

. . .

"As you walk along beside the water's edge, you are followed by ducks that waddle along hoping for some food."

. . .

"There are many kinds of birds living near this lake and you can hear them singing and calling to each other. What kinds of birds live near your lake? Some of these water birds will be quite different from the ones that live in your magical rainforest. What colors are their feathers? What noises are they making?"

. . .

"As you come to the water's edge, you see a boat, a safety vest, and a paddle. The boat is waiting for you to get in and make your way out onto the water. It is very easy to drift along in the boat. The water and the gentle breeze are helping you move along the rippling current."

. . .

"Spend some time here, just enjoying the feeling of floating on the water and taking in the beauty and relaxation that nature gives us."

. . .

"Do you see any fish swimming in the lake? Are there any birds flying overhead? Have the ducks paddled out onto the lake with you?"

. . .

"Begin to paddle back to the water's edge and leave your boat on the small beach beside the lake. It will be waiting there for you when next you return to this wonderful, peaceful place."

. . .

"Now, walk back through the garden and into our room. How do you feel after your journey to the lake? Try to think of a word that describes how you feel right now."

. . .

"Now gently move your body in the way that you like to bring yourself out of your relaxation state. When your eyes are open and you are sitting up, we'll spend some time talking about our special boat trip on the lake . . ."

Relaxation sessions can be concluded by having the children form a "sharing circle," where each child talks about their tai chi and relaxation/ visualization experience. As part of the discussion that takes place after relaxation practice, it is important to point out to children that when they are more calm and relaxed, they can approach their worries or fears from a more balanced perspective and act to create a solution rather than react and create a bigger problem.

This is a good opportunity to develop listening, sharing, and kindness skills. Children learn to be polite and respectful to each other, understanding that each person's contribution is valuable, even if it is different from their own. The children can describe their favorite tai chi movement and tell the group what they "saw" on their imaginary journey.

It is important for the educator or parent to be open to all ideas and imaginings offered by the children. Similarly, children who do not wish to share their thoughts and feelings on any particular day should be acknowledged and feel free to simply "be" and listen to the others for a while.

CHAPTER 6

Creative Expression

Relaxation exercises can form an effective part of movement experiences for young children. Alternating vigorous, fast-paced activities with quieter ones helps children remain calm and avoids "bouncing off the walls." Relaxation helps children prepare for slow and sustained movement, which requires greater control than fast movement. There is a wealth of ways to bring the lessons of peace, quiet, and the reflections gained from relaxation into other areas of the curricula. Tai chi and relaxation sessions can be followed up with a range of creative and expressive experiences such as the following:

- ❖ Drawing
- ❖ Painting
- ❖ Patterning
- ❖ Modeling with clay or plasticine
- ❖ Story writing
- ❖ Dancing
- ❖ Drama activities
- ❖ Music

Possibilities for following up on relaxation sessions are only limited by the imaginations of the teacher or parent and the children. The following illustrations show some of the stories and drawings created by children after their relaxation sessions.

"I'm floating on a cloud going to the hundred-acre wood where my birthday party is going to be. I feel very happy."
(Boy aged four years)

"It's me rowing a boat. I'm just about to get out of the boat and put my feet in the water. This is my boat in relaxation."
(Girl aged three and a half years)

"My head is popping over to see if my hands are doing the right thing in tai chi." (Boy aged four years)

"My garden is on the mountain." (Boy aged six years)

"Me painting the rainbow." (Boy aged four years)

"I like tai chi because it's good." (Boy aged four years)

"Relaxed." (Boy aged five years)

Life learning   Relaxation time can impart important social learning. The following ideas help children build connection, understanding, and respect for each other and their world:

- ❖ Listening (poems, stories, rhymes, songs)
- ❖ Sharing/waiting/respecting/kindness activities
- ❖ Valuing nature (outdoor relaxation activities)
- ❖ Just "being"

Creative expression   Relaxation time can lead children to a wealth of opportunities to explore and develop through the creative and expressive arts. The following are some examples of ways children can represent their relaxation and tai chi experiences:

- ❖ Drawing
- ❖ Painting
- ❖ Patterning
- ❖ Modeling
- ❖ Collage
- ❖ Sculpture
- ❖ Drama
- ❖ Dancing
- ❖ Storytelling
- ❖ Poems and rhymes
- ❖ Constructing

Aromatherapy and simple massage can also be used if appropriate and if in accordance with policy and guidelines if in an education setting.

GENERAL IDEAS FOR BABIES, TODDLERS, AND OLDER CHILDREN   This book follows a specific program of relaxation by starting with warm-up movements, tai chi, and gentle exercises. Progressive relaxation is then followed by visualization techniques and group discussion of the children's responses. Creative expression activities are then suggested to explore and record the relaxation techniques further. However, there is a range of general ideas that can be used with children that may help "set the scene" before you embark on the program. These ideas can also be used in addition to the relaxation sessions outlined in the book.

The following ideas may be used with babies. Experiment with these ideas *Babies* and watch baby's reactions. Include the following suggestions, along with more ideas of your own:

- Use relaxation music in their rooms (lullabies, nature sounds, quiet chants, and soft ambient music)
- Use aesthetics to enhance the environment (soft colors, attractive posters, mobiles, hangings, a relaxation mat with soft toys for soothing activities inside and outdoors)
- Make sure adults use relaxed, calm voices
- Try aromatherapy, such as oil burners, scented lights, and mist sprays—make sure you research this for contraindications before you use this technique
- Use massage at diaper-changing time, bath time, rest, or sleep time
- Read stories to babies as they sit on your lap
- Use chewing/soothing toys
- Use plenty of cuddles, swaying, and rocking

Use the above ideas suggested for babies as well as the following ones with *Toddlers* toddlers. Play with these techniques and modify them according to your toddlers' responses:

- Use music in their rooms (ambient, light classical, relaxation, nature sounds, chanting, lullabies, and multicultural)
- Use aesthetics (soft furnishings, quiet corners, posters, plants, mobiles, book areas, cushions, soft toys, draping fabrics, lamps for soft lighting, aromatherapy, float bowls, flowers, and plants)
- Use movement to create breaks in your day (for example, before or after toileting time, snack time, recess, moving to another

room or activity, lunch—try tai chi, bending and stretching, circle dancing, creative dancing, yoga)

◈ Use relaxing activities (a relaxation mat outside for quiet drawing or playing with soft toys, sand trays, water play, bubbles, private space and time, cubbies, using the garden, relaxation and spiritual books, and transition times)

◈ Use tactile experiences (sand, water, goop, slime, dough)

◈ Read stories to toddlers as they sit on your lap

Older Children   The above ideas can be extended for use with older children. To the items in the infant and toddler lists above, you might add some of the ideas in the following list when developing relaxation ideas for preschool and school-aged children:

◈ Extended movement and exercise (breathing, warm-ups, tai chi, yoga)

◈ Progressive relaxation—learning to relax the body systematically with the breath, valuing sitting or lying still, and "just being"; quiet time for music appreciation

◈ Visualization—creating images in our minds to help us relax, making our own relaxation symbol, making up our own relaxation and visualization "scripts"

◈ Listening to extended or serial stories or chapter books

◈ Self-massage—learning to stroke hands and face, gentle circles at back of neck, head, and lower back

◈ Music and rhythm activities reflecting visualization themes using percussion instruments, soft drumming, or rhythm sticks

◈ Exploring textures and patterns in a range of materials—scarves, cushions, pieces of fabric that are soft and silky to touch; wool and silk for their comforting, soothing, and aesthetic qualities

◈ Developing human awareness and environmental awareness activities and exploring the interrelationship between the two—for example, relaxation activities outside such as lying down on the grass for a cloud visualization; making a "secret" garden at school based on relaxation and meditation themes; texture touching activities outside; exploring environmental shapes, colors, and textures; tree hug; exploring sounds; pet rocks; observation games; environmental I-spy and bingo games—all of these increase knowledge and awareness of self and environment

CONCLUSION

Relaxation is a life skill that is just as important as all the other skills children learn in preschool and school, if not more important. The ideas contained within this book are designed as a resource and a springboard to further relaxation activities. Adults and children can develop these activities together. It is my belief that the earlier we incorporate "heart and soul" learning into our curricula—that is, learning how to relax, be calm, content, and at peace with oneself—the better life will be for the children in our care.

Learning to relax does not come easily for many adults, so we cannot expect children to learn these skills immediately. It takes time and effort to learn to relax our minds, bodies, and spirits through the tai chi and relaxation techniques offered in this book.

Life is fast paced and stressful for many children. The ideas in this book will help children and adults manage their stresses in positive and gentle ways. However, this book is not meant to be a "fix it" type of manual. It is my hope that we can teach children how to relax, be calm, breathe easily, visualize wondrous images, and accept themselves and others at an early age. In this way children can be, in some ways, prepared for stress and upset when it inevitably occurs. Many conflicts, worries, illnesses, and times of grief unexpectedly appear in all our lives. Many adults struggle to find ways to help them through these uninvited and often unthinkable times. We are often left grasping for reassurance, comfort, peace, and inner strength on these occasions. This book will help our children learn to "act" in positive ways rather than "react" to their environment and those around them. I see the learning of these skills as creating an armory that we can use when we are challenged or find ourselves off balance in life.

As well as calling on relaxation skills in troubled times, children can learn positive habits early in their lives and experience the richness and creativity of a fluid, graceful body and an imaginative, active mind. I hope these skills will one day replace some of the mind-numbing and violent activity children witness on television and in video games. If we wish for our children to have hope, optimism, and fulfilment in their lives, we surely must help them by paving the way with ideas and practices that enhance these values. The alternative is a life of intellectual and personal mediocrity and impoverishment.

If we care enough about the health, happiness, and well-being of our children, we will make a commitment to incorporate some of the ideas in this book into the daily lives of our children.

> For the cause of
> worldwide peace and harmony
> May it begin in the
> Hearts of children
> And spread.
> *(Fields and Boesser 1994, iv)*

Supplemental Materials for Working with Other Adults

How can this book help me in my work with children?
The relaxation skills outlined in this book integrate the physical, intellectual, social, emotional, and spiritual potentials of children so that they can become more responsive to their environment. School and early childhood centers are currently undergoing rapid change . . . not all good in my view. Overemphasis on competency-based learning and overreliance on technology are two examples of this change. I believe it is time to bring relaxation skills into wide use in our schools and homes.

How can I fit relaxation time into my busy schedule?
It may be time to reorder your priorities. Are there any routines or less beneficial activities that could be dispensed with? For example, the relaxation program is a perfect substitute for rest or nap time for those children who have grown out of the need to sleep during the day. Do you waste time "managing" the behavior of your children? Inclusion of short relaxation times during the day may work as a preventative measure to behavior problems in some children. The children are settled and focused after a relaxation session. Use this as a prelude to experiences that will require focus and concentration. The visualization exercises are a wonderful springboard for imaginative storytelling and writing, creative expression, and communication activities with peers.

Are relaxation techniques "New Age" or religious concepts?
Although tai chi is derived from Eastern traditions, the movements, as they are presented in this book, do not promote any religious beliefs. I

have been invited to present tai chi and relaxation sessions to a range of schools and centers to children and staff with diverse religious backgrounds or no religious background whatsoever.

As health and meditative practices from a wide range of traditions are becoming more mainstream in Australian and American culture, this concern is becoming less prevalent. Inform parents and colleagues about the program by keeping the lines of communication open—hold information evenings, provide written information, photographs, and even video footage of the children learning the techniques. Discuss the lifelong benefits of tai chi (or any other gentle exercise), relaxation, and visualization techniques.

Nonetheless, an individual's or parent's right not to participate in the program or not to have their children participate should always be respected.

Tai chi exercises are only suitable for adults.
This book proves otherwise! Reassure families that tai chi exercises are safe and noninvasive. As mentioned throughout, these techniques have been used for many years by my colleagues and me across diverse age ranges and settings for children. Show them a copy of this book!

The staff members do not know how to do the tai chi or relaxation exercises.
No one needs to be an expert to teach tai chi or relaxation to children. After all, we teach music, but many of us are not musicians; we teach drama, but many of us are not actors. Learn with the children by following the guidelines in this book. Educators are constantly turning to books and other resources to learn new games, dances, songs, rhymes and poems, science experiments, sporting techniques, and drama ideas. It is no different for relaxation techniques. Just give it a go—you'll soon become hooked!

What should I do if the children act "silly" when I'm trying to get these activities going?
First, you need to be relaxed and at ease—remember, stressed adults cannot help children to learn to relax! Check that you have followed the implementation guidelines set out in this book. Think of how you would deal with silliness during other activities. Would you use an "I-message" to remind the children of your expectations? For example, "It is disappointing when people misbehave during relaxation. Let's all listen and enjoy this time together."

When relaxation activities are introduced to children for the first time, there can be a testing of the waters. The techniques bring with them their own appeal, calm, and discipline in a short space of time. The initial silliness will subside. I know this from my rich experiences over the years with children with emotional and behavioral disabilities.

Of course, all children have bad days. Occasionally a child may just want to sit and watch. They may wish to quietly look at a book on this occasion. Be clear that they are not to disrupt the relaxation enjoyment of their classmates. If a child is particularly angry or upset on any one day, it may be helpful to ask a colleague or parent to undertake another activity with the child away from the group. Teamwork and support for each other help the relaxation program to succeed.

What should I call these activities?
Ask your children to help you choose a name. In my research, I have discovered a wealth of ideas, from "relaxation time," "meditation time," "awareness activities," "centering activities," and "quiet time" through to "Kiddie Quieting Reflex" and "Head Ed." (The last two are not my favorites!)

Should we hold a discussion after each session?
It's up to you. Try not to force a lesson to be learned from each session—that is not the point of the program. It is important, however, to allow children time to debrief from their experiences and share their responses (if they choose to) with their peers.

Will I encounter resistance from my management committee, director, principal, or school board?
Clearly, you need to seek permission from supervisors and parents before embarking on a relaxation program. Most often, they will be excited about the possibilities a relaxation program represents. Providing information about the benefits of such a program is always a good start. This book and the references cited at the end will provide ample background reading.

HOW MUCH DAILY RELAXATION TIME
DO YOUR CHILDREN HAVE?

(This does not mean time in front of the television or computer games!)

A Checklist for Parents

It's important for children to have quiet time each day, where they can just "be" without expectations, noise, or activity. Sometimes we push our children too hard and they can suffer from overload.

. . . .

- ❧ How much time is devoted to relaxation activities for your children each day?

- ❧ Are your children overscheduled? Extracurricular activities can be enjoyable and beneficial; however, too many commitments to sports, tutoring, music, dance classes, and so on, can be overwhelming for children.

- ❧ Do your children have difficulty in remembering which activities they need to attend? Has "looking forward" to an activity been replaced by a feeling of obligation?

- ❧ Is there time for your children to play each day? This does not just mean the very young. All children need to be engaged in fun activities—play, socializing, and just "hanging out" with friends—for healthy, balanced development.

- ❧ Do your children have ongoing projects and hobbies at home? Is there a sense of wonder, curiosity, and keen problem solving evident in activities around your home?

RELAXATION AT HOME

Why use relaxation techniques at home?

In today's fast-paced society, stress is becoming an ever-increasing problem for children. Children have become the unintended victims of constantly being hurried. Relaxation techniques provide key life competencies for children's health and well-being. We need to increase children's repertoire of coping skills so that they can positively respond to life's demands and challenges. Relaxation skills develop positive behaviors. When children learn how to make their bodies and minds become calm and peaceful, they are producing constructive and positive ways of dealing with life.

Children need to be reminded that they have wonderful bodies that need time for rest and replenishment . . . and that their bodies need to be treated gently. Relaxation helps the body, the mind, and the emotions all work together in gentle harmony.

How does relaxation help children?

Relaxation helps children in these ways:

- Relaxes the body
- Quiets the mind
- Allows the child to "be"
- Provides rest and rejuvenation
- Develops coping skills
- Enhances self-awareness
- Provides time-out and solitude

How can I help my children cope with stress?

Remember, stressed adults cannot help children to learn to relax. Learn to recognize your stress reactions and develop ways of bringing relaxation, peace, calm, and replenishment into your daily life. Children learn from watching what we do and will be encouraged to try some relaxation techniques if they observe parents looking after themselves in positive ways.

Here are some ways to help yourself develop a more relaxed way of being:

- ❖ Use breathing techniques
- ❖ Make time for meditation, prayer, or reflection
- ❖ Get regular exercise
- ❖ Use affirmations
- ❖ Nurture yourself
- ❖ Develop a beautiful and serene home and work environment

What will my family gain from relaxation times together?
Here are some of the benefits other families have observed:

- ❖ Greater communication
- ❖ Positive time together that transforms the stresses of the day into vitality, energy, and enchantment with life
- ❖ Greater understanding of each family member's thoughts, feelings, and imaginings
- ❖ Recognition of the value of quiet, peaceful times spent together where *being* is more important than *doing*
- ❖ New ways of caring for and nurturing each other
- ❖ Respect and understanding for the value of each person's inner life
- ❖ Ways to deal with life's challenges, sadness, trauma, and disappointments while empowering each person in the family

How can I begin using relaxation in my family life?
Set up a special relaxation area in your home and set the scene by decorating it with flowers, candles, plants, posters, a flower or candle floating in a bowl of water, crystals, shells, or any objects that you or your children choose to enhance the feeling of relaxation.

What does a family relaxation time look like?
You can use the suggestions in *The Power of Relaxation* or other books featuring gentle stretching, yoga, or tai chi. Start by doing a few warm-ups together followed by a few gentle exercises. You may wish to have your child lie down on the floor and take them through progressive relaxation (tensing and relaxing each of the muscle groups in the body sequentially), or use a visualization script. These tools are both described in *The Power of Relaxation* and other books on relaxation and visualization.

You may even wish to make an audiotape of your voice reading the relaxation instructions or visualization script so that you can lie down and enjoy the experience along with your child. Play relaxing music in the background. Remember to bring your child out of the relaxation state slowly. You may want to do a few stretches together to get your bodies moving again.

You might follow up your relaxation techniques with a sharing time where each family member discusses their experiences and feelings during the session. Drawing pictures, working with playdough or clay, writing stories (for older children), and painting are all ways of sharing the relaxation experience.

What else can I do to help my child become more relaxed?
Here are a selection of exercises that you can use during a family relaxation time, or any time you want to help children let go of stress.

1. Practice making the body tight, then relaxed (loose and floppy). To help children deepen their ability to relax their bodies, ask them to imagine that their bodies are like one of these things:

   ◈ An ice cream that is slowly melting
   ◈ A wobbly jellyfish
   ◈ A cat sleeping in the sun
   ◈ A puppet with loose strings

2. Have children stretch their bodies in various ways:

   ◈ Reaching the arms above the head
   ◈ Stretching sideways
   ◈ Stretching the arms out in front
   ◈ Stretching and imagining the children are climbing a ladder

3. Use five-minute relaxations. With children sitting cross-legged or lying down, ask them to breathe easily and evenly as follows:

   ◈ Count 1: Breathe in
   ◈ Count 2: Breathe out
   ◈ Count 3: Breathe in

Continue slowly counting breaths until the child appears more calm and relaxed. This can be followed by the child imagining a favorite relaxation image and holding it for a few minutes. For example, ask the child to imagine a beautiful tree, fish swimming in a tank, a bright star, glowing embers in a fire, a soft cloud, a leaf drifting in the wind, gentle waves lapping on the shore, and so on.

4. Use a walking relaxation exercise to coordinate the mind and body and replenish children's energy if they are out of sorts. Take a short walk with your child, perhaps around the block. Breathe evenly and walk briskly while swinging your arms back and forth. When the left foot steps forward, the right arm swings forward and vice versa. Focus on the breath while walking in this rhythm. You will feel much more refreshed after this activity.

5. Collect natural items for a treasure box. Spend some time outdoors with your child collecting valued treasures (driftwood, dried flowers, shiny pebbles, feathers, leaves, and so on) to keep in a box (which you and your child can decorate). This box of treasures can be a resource when setting up the relaxation area at home.

6. Create a worry tree. Talk to your child about anything that is worrying her, and write the worries down on pieces of colored paper. Hang them on a small tree branch collected from the garden so that the child can be "free" of them for a while.

REFERENCES

Below is a list of books and articles I use in my work with children and adults. A few may seem a little dated, but the ideas and information they contain are nevertheless valuable.

Alister, K. 1998. Weaving the magic circle: Teaching spirituality to children. *Insight* (January) 14–15.

Amorsen, A. 2002. Supporting stressed children. *Wellbeing Magazine Annual,* (86), 62–65.

Anderson, B. 1997. *Stretching at your computer desk.* Bolinas, Calif.: Shelter Publications.

Armstrong, T. 1995. *The myth of the A.D.D. child.* New York: Plume.

Australian Bureau of Statistics. 2002. *AusStats.* <http://www.abs.gov.au>.

Bennett, V. 1996. *Making dreams come true: Visualisations and practical exercises to help children set and achieve their goals.* Sydney: Hodder and Stoughton.

———. 2001. *Lifesmart: Choices for young people about friendship, family, and future.* Sydney: Finch Publishing.

Blumenfield, L., ed. 1995. *The big book of relaxation.* Adelaide: Brolga Publishing.

Campbell, S., T. Castelino, M. Coady, H. Lawrence, G. MacNaughton, S. Rolfe, K. Smith, and J. Totta. 2001. *Our part in peace.* Canberra: Australian Early Childhood Association (AECA).

Catalfo, P. 1997. *Raising spiritual children in a material world.* New York: Berkeley Books.

Chuen, L. K. 1999. *The way of healing: Chi kung for energy and health.* London: Axiom.

Crompton, P. 1996. *Tai chi: A practical introduction to the therapeutic effects of the discipline.* London: Quarto Publishing.

Crook, R. 1988. *Relaxation for children.* Katoomba: Second Back Row Publishing.

Dacey, J., and L. Fiore. 2002. *Your anxious child: How parents and teachers can relieve anxiety in children.* San Francisco: Jossey Bass.

Dang, T. 1994. *Beginning tai chi.* Boston: Charles E. Tuttle.

Doe, M., and M. Walch. 1998. *101 principles for spiritual parenting.* New York: Harper Collins.

Eastman, M. 1994. *Taming the dragon in your child.* New York: John Wiley and Sons.

Elkind, D. 1988. *The hurried child: Growing up too fast too soon.* Rev. ed. Reading, Mass.: Addison Wesley.

Farhi, D. 1996. *The breathing book.* New York: Henry Holt.

Farmer, S. 1989. Stress—Kids are vulnerable too. *Rattler* 11 (Spring).

Field, E. 1999. *Bullying busting: How to help children deal with teasing and bullying.* Sydney: Finch Publishing.

Field, V., and P. Thomas. 2002. *Tai chi: Advancing health into the 21st century.* Paper presented at 4th annual Allied Health Conference, Royal Hospital for Women, Randwick, December.

Fields, M., and C. Boesser. 1994. *Constructive guidance and discipline.* New York: Macmillan.

Fontana, D. 2002. *The meditator's handbook.* London: Thorsons.

Fontana, D., and I. Slack. 2002. *Teaching meditation to children.* London: Thorsons.

Furman, R. 1995. Helping children cope with stress and deal with feelings. *Young Children* 50 (2): 33–41.

Galante, L. 1981. *Tai Chi: The supreme ultimate.* New York: Samuel Weiser.

Garth, M. 1991. *Starbright.* San Francisco: HarperSanFrancisco.

———. 1997. *Earthlight.* San Francisco: HarperSanFrancisco.

Gawler, I. 1989. *Peace of mind.* New York: Avery Penguin Putnam.

George, M. 1998. *Learn to relax: A practical guide to easing tension and conquering stress.* San Francisco: Chronicle.

Goleman, D. 1988. *The meditative mind.* Los Angeles: Tarcher.

Greenman, J. 2002. *What happened to the world: Helping children cope in turbulent times.* Sydney: Pademelon Press.

Hay, L. 1984. *You can heal your life.* Santa Monica, Calif.: Hay House.

Hayes, R. D. n.d. Fast Forward? Working longer, harder, and for less in the 24/7 economy. <http://www.ilwu.org/1099/fastforward-1099.htm> (2003).

Hendricks, G., and R. Wills. 1975. *The centering book.* Englewood Cliffs, N.J.: Prentice Hall.

———. 1977. *The second centering book.* Englewood Cliffs, N.J.: Prentice Hall.

Hewitt, D., and S. Heidemann. 1998. *The optimistic classroom: Creative ways to give children hope.* St. Paul: Redleaf Press.

Honig, A. 1986. Research in review: Stress and coping in children. In *Reducing stress in young children's lives,* edited by Brown McCracken. Washington: NAEYC.

Hutchinson, F. 1996. *Educating beyond violent futures.* New York: Routledge.

International Labour Survey. 1999.

Jacka, J. 1990. *Meditation.* Melbourne: Lothian.

Jacobsen, E. 1938. *Progressive relaxation.* Chicago: University of Chicago Press.

———. 1970. *You must relax.* New York: McGraw Hill.

Jahnke, R. 2002. *The healing promise of Qi: Creating extraordinary wellness through qigong and tai chi.* New York: Contemporary Books.

Jenkins, P. 1995. *Nurturing spirituality in children.* Hillsboro, Oreg.: Beyond Words Publishing.

Jones, M. 1999. *Your Child—Headaches and migraine: Practical and easy to follow advice.* Shaftesbury: Element Books.

———. 2000. *Hyperactivity: What's the alternative?* Shaftesbury: Element Books.

Kent, H. 1997. *Breathe better, feel better: Learn to increase your energy, control anxiety and anger, relieve health problems, and just relax with simple breathing techniques.* Allentown, Pa.: People's Medical Society.

Kersey, K. 1986. *Helping your child handle stress.* Washington, D.C.: Acropolis Books.

Khor, G. 1993. *Tai chi: Qigong for stress control and relaxation.* Sydney: Simon and Schuster.

Lane-Smith, S. 2000. *Calm kids: Using alternative therapies to give your child the gift of inner peace.* Melbourne: Thomas C. Lothian.

Lewis, D. 1996. *I close my eyes and I see.* Findhorn, Scotland: Findhorn Press.

Lynch, J., and C. Huang. 1999. *Working out, working within: The Tao of inner fitness through sport and exercise.* New York: Tarcher/Putnam.

McKinnon, P. 1991. *Helping yourself and your child to happiness.* Melbourne: David Lovell.

McKissock, D. 1998. *The grief of our children.* Sydney: ABC Books.

Madders, J. 1987. *Relax and be happy.* New York: HarperCollins.

Merson, J. 2001. *Stress: The causes, the costs, and the cures.* Sydney: ABC Books.

Miller, K. 1996. *The crisis manual for early childhood teachers: How to handle the really difficult problems.* Beltsville, Md.: Gryphon House.

Milne, R. 1997. *Peace education in early childhood.* Richmond, Victoria: The Free Kindergarten Association.

Moore, T. 1997. *The education of the heart.* New York: Perennial.

Nagy, L. 1995. *The natural choice guide to aromatherapy.* Sydney: Hodder & Stoughton.

National Center for Health Statistics. 2000. Prevalence of overweight and obesity among adults: United States, 1999–2000. <http://www.cdc.gov/nchs/products/pubs/pubd/hestats/obese/obse99.htm>.

———. 2000. Prevalence of overweight and obesity among children and adolescents: United States, 1999–2000. <www.cdc.gov/nchs/products/pubs/pubd/hestats.overwght99.htm>.

National Institute of Mental Health. 2001. The numbers count. <http://www.nimh.nih.gov>.

Neville, B. 1989. *Educating psyche.* Melbourne: Collins Dove.

Odle, C. 1990. *Practical visualisation.* London: Aquarian.

Pearson, M. 1998. *Emotional healing and self-esteem.* Melbourne: Australian Council for Education Research (ACER).

Pearson, M., and P. Nolan. 1991. *Emotional first aid for children.* Springwood: Butterfly Press.

Pica, R. 1995. *Experiences in movement.* New York: Delmar.

Porter, L. 1999. *Young children's behaviour: Practical approaches for caregivers and teachers.* Sydney: MacLennan and Petty.

Proto, L. 1990. *Self healing.* London: Judy Piatkus.

Reid, H. 1989. *The way of harmony.* New York: Fireside.

Rice, J. 1995. *The kindness curriculum: Introducing young children to loving values.* St. Paul: Redleaf Press.

Rice, P. 1999. *Stress and health.* Pacific Grove, Calif.: Brooks/Cole.

Richardson, G. 1998. *Love as conscious action.* Sydney: Gavemer Publishing.

Rickard, J. 1996. *Relaxation for children.* Sterling, Va.: Stylus Publishing.

Roe, D. 1996. *Young children and stress: How can we help?* Canberra: AECA.

Romano, J. 1992. Psychoeducational interventions for stress management and well-being. *Journal of Counseling and Development* 64 (5): 31–32.

Rozman, D. 2002. *Meditating with children.* Buckingham, Va.: Integral Yoga Distribution.

Saavedra, B. 1999. *Creating balance in your child's life.* Chicago: Contemporary Books.

Sanders, T., ed. 1997. *Foods that harm, foods that heal.* Pleasantville, N.Y.: Reader's Digest.

Shepherd, W., and J. Eaton. 1997. Creating environments that intrigue and delight children and adults. *Child Care Information Exchange* 9 (97): 42–7.

Stewart, M., and K. Phillips. 1993. *Yoga for children: Simple exercises to help children grow strong and supple.* New York: Fireside.

Stukin, S. 2001. Om Schooling. *Yoga Journal* (November): 89–93, 151–53.

Thomas, P. 1994. *Learning for the heart and soul*. Master's thesis, University of Sydney.

Thomas, P., and W. Shepherd. 2000. Relaxation: Every child's right to simply be. *Child Care Information Exchange* 1 (131): 42–8.

Uhlmann, L. 1997. Meditation for children. *Wellbeing Magazine* (69) 24.

U.S. Census Bureau. 2000. *Census 2000*. <http://census.gov>.

U.S. Department of Education. 1999. National Household Education Survey. <http://www.ed.gov>.

U.S. Department of Health and Human Services. n.d. Mental health: A report of the Surgeon General. <http://www.surgeongeneral.gov>.

———. 1999. Physical activity and health: A report of the Surgeon General. <www.cdc.gov/nccdphp/sgr/sgr.htm>.

Walker, P. 1985. *Baby relax*. London: Unwin.

Wellisch, M. 2000. *Games children play: The effects of media violence on young children*. AECA Research in Practice Series, 7 (2).

Wiles, Susan. 1981. *Tai chi*. Chicago: Contemporary Books.

Wolf, A. 2000. How to nurture the spirit in nonsectarian environments. *Young Children* 55 (1): 34–36.

Youngs, B. 1995. *Stress and your child: Helping kids cope with the strains and pressures of life*. New York: Fawcett Books.

Zhuo, D. 1984. *The Chinese exercise book*. Emmaus, Pa.: Rodale.

MUSIC SELECTIONS

There is a wealth of ambient, nature, classical, and relaxation music available—these are a few of my favorites.

3 Roses. Dale Nougher. 1994. Larrikin Entertainment.

Australian Lullaby. Tony O'Connor. 1988. Studio Horizon Productions. <http://www.tonyo'connor.com.au>

Dream and Discoveries. Tony O'Connor. 1999. Studio Horizon Productions. <http://www.tonyo'connor.com.au>

Dreamtime. Tony O'Connor. 1999. Studio Horizon Productions. <http://www.tonyo'connor.com.au>

Heart and Soul. 1997. Rhythmist Productions. <http://www.iancameronsmith.com.au>

Inner Tides. Ian Cameron Smith. 1994. Rhythmist Productions. <http://www.iancameronsmith.com.au>

In Touch. Tony O'Connor. 1999. Studio Horizon Productions. <http://www.tonyo'connor.com.au>

Lunar Reflections. Ian Cameron Smith. 1993. Rhythmist Productions. <http://www.iancameronsmith.com.au>

Mariner. Tony O'Connor. 1990. Studio Horizon Productions. <http://www.tonyo'connor.com.au>

Medicine Woman. Medwyn Goodall. 1992. New World Productions.

Music for Mother and Child. Tony O'Connor. 1999. Studio Horizon Productions. <http://www.tonyo'connor.com.au>

Rainforest Magic. Tony O'Connor. 1991. Studio Horizon Productions. <http://www.tonyo'connor.com.au>

Rockpool Reflections. Andrew Skeoch. 1994. Listening Earth Productions.

Tales of the Wind. Tony O'Connor. 1991. Studio Horizon Productions. <http://www.tonyo'connor.com.au>

Uluru. Tony O'Connor. 1991. Studio Horizon Productions.

White Winds. Andreas Vollenwieder. 1984. CBS.

OTHER RESOURCES FROM REDLEAF PRESS

Star Power for Preschoolers: Learning Life Skills through Physical Play
by Andrew Oser
Physical play helps young children develop five life success skills: self-esteem, concentration, imagination, cooperation, and relaxation. More than 60 group games and movement activities will help children develop these skills.

Hollyhocks and Honeybees: Garden Projects for Young Children
by Sara Starbuck, Marla Olthof, and Karen Midden
This practical guide introduces teachers—with or without green thumbs—to the rich learning opportunities found in gardening with children.

Making it Better: Activities for Children Living in a Stressful World
by Barbara Oehlberg
This important book offers bold new information about the physical and emotional effects of stress, trauma, and violence on children today and gives teachers and caregivers the confidence to help children survive, thrive, and learn.

The Optimistic Classroom: Creative Ways to Give Children Hope
by Deborah Hewitt and Sandra Heidemann
Over seventy activities will develop ten strengths that allow children to meet and cope with the challenges they face.

More Than…Series
by Sally Moomaw and Brenda Hieronymus
This popular series is an integrated curriculum for five important areas of early learning: math, art, music, science, and reading and writing. Each book in the series offers answers to questions that teachers often ask and includes complete directions and illustrations for over 100 hands-on activities.

More Than Singing: Discovering Music in Preschool and Kindergarten
by Sally Moomaw
More than 100 activities and ideas for songs, instrument making, music centers, and extensions into language, science, and math. Clear directions and musical notations guide you.

Designs for Living and Learning: Transforming Early Childhood Environments
by Deb Curtis and Margie Carter
Drawing inspiration from a variety of approaches, from Waldorf to Montessori and Reggio to Greenman, Prescott, and Olds, *Designs for Living and Learning* outlines hundreds of ways to create healthy and inviting physical, social, and emotional environments for children in child care.

800-423-8309
www.redleafpress.org